LETTE
TO
CHANGE
THE
WORLD

LETTERS TO CHANGE THE WORLD

From
EMMELINE PANKHURST
to **MARTIN LUTHER KING, JR.**

Edited by Travis Elborough

3
Ebury Press, an imprint of Ebury Publishing
20 Vauxhall Bridge Road
London SW1V 2SA

Ebury Press is part of the Penguin Random House Group of companies
whose addresses can be found at global.penguinrandomhouse.com

First published by Ebury Press in 2018
This edition published by Ebury Press in 2021
www.penguin.co.uk

A CIP catalogue record for this book is available from the British Library

ISBN 9781529109948

Typeset in 10.23/12.98 pt Bembo Std by Jouve (UK), Milton Keynes

Printed and bound in Great Britain by Clays Ltd, Elcograf S.p.A.

The authorised representative in the EEA is Penguin Random House
Ireland, Morrison Chambers, 32 Nassau Street, Dublin D02 YH68.

Contents

Introduction

At a time when the liberties we often take for granted seem to be under threat, *Letters to Change the World* is intended to offer reminders from history that, if we want to change the world, standing up for and voicing our personal and political beliefs is both a right and a duty.

From William Wilberforce and Emmeline Pankhurst through to Nelson Mandela and Ziauddin Yousafzai, father of Malala, many of the letters collected here are penned by major figures from the world stage. Poets, writers and thinkers such as Leo Tolstoy, Bertrand Russell, Wilfred Owen, Doris Lessing and Alice Walker have also been included, while other letters are written by ordinary citizens caught up in history by their pursuit of what is right. The little-known and downright obscure also take their place here among the great and the good – the former have often achieved great things by the simple act of putting pen to paper. The fight for the right to work and to be respected whatever your gender, sexuality or skin colour has long been a battle of words. That the personal *is* political is hopefully writ large across these pages. Printed discourse is good for democracy; we need to talk openly and honestly to each other to avoid totalitarianism in all its stripes, and to speak truth to power when we see it being abused.

Our collection begins in the eighteenth century, the era of the Enlightenment but also of 'Rotten Boroughs', transatlantic slavery and punitive penal codes, when the majority of the world's population remained disenfranchised. And the book's finale finds us in the contemporary age of digital 'clicktivism' and online petitions where, perhaps against all expectations, the open letter, a form so beloved of the coffee-house radicals and bar-room revolutionaries of yesteryear, has been reborn. History, it would appear, genuinely favours the epistolary. Ink and paper might be absent from many modern-day calls for action, but their sentiments are surely no less worthy or necessary. The 'gig' economy and the insecure nature of work for the 'precariat', and present-day, even 'everyday' sexism, homophobia and racial prejudice are sadly not without their precedents, as the odd example here shows, though others provide more reassuring evidence of the valiant gains made in the intervening decades and centuries. But over a century since the suffragettes, #MeToo and Time's Up tell us there is far more work yet to do.

Inevitably there are absences and omissions. Still, we believe there is enough ammunition in this anthology to encourage those who dream of improving the world to wield their pens (or keyboards, phones and iPads) ever mightier than swords, and change the world for the better.

Editor's Note

Letters have been edited in places for length, clarity and sense but where possible the authors' spellings and grammar have been retained to remain as true as possible to the original correspondence.

1.
Olaudah Equiano's Letter to Queen Charlotte on Slavery, 1788

Incomprehensible as it might seem to us now, at the time of Olaudah Equiano's birth in around 1745, the trafficking of human beings, mostly from Africa to the Americas and the Caribbean, was largely considered by the free as an unremarkable fact of life. History was on their side: slavery had been practised by the earliest human civilisations, including such pioneers of democratic government as the Ancient Greeks. Even more horrifyingly, it remains with us today. But, in Britain, in the latter half of the eighteenth century, many prominent voices began to raise their voices against slavery on moral and religious grounds. Figures including the Anglican Cambridge scholar Thomas Clarkson, the civil servant Granville Sharp, the parliamentarian William Wilberforce, the pottery manufacturer Josiah Wedgwood, and William Allen, a Quaker silk maker and scientist who forswore sugar (one the chief products of slave labour) for over forty years, became leading lights in the 'Society for Effecting the Abolition of the Slave Trade'. This organisation, formed in 1787, is justly celebrated for its pivotal role in the campaign to end the sale of human beings as chattel across Britain's colonial territories. Fundamental to that cause, however, was the contribution and testimony of an associated group of freed former slaves in London, known as 'the Sons of Africa'. One of their most active founding members was Olaudah Equiano.

Historians and scholars have contested Equiano's origins in recent decades, with some evidence suggesting his birthplace was quite possibly South Carolina in America, rather than the Eboe province of today's southern Nigeria, as he had claimed in his phenomenally successful self-published autobiography, *The Interesting Narrative of the Life of Olaudah Equiano, or Gustavus Vassa, the African*. In the book, he recounts movingly his alleged kidnap and sale into slavery at the age of eleven, and his shipping to Barbados and Virginia. While questions remain over the veracity of certain elements of his life story, Equiano certainly knew first-hand what it was like to live as an enslaved person who could be bought and resold at the drop of a hat, unable even to choose or keep one's own name. The British Naval Officer Michael Henry Pascal acquired Equiano in 1756 and renamed him against his wishes after Gustav Vassa, the sixteenth century Swedish king. With Pascal, and as a slave, Equiano sailed on many voyages around the world. A decade later, having been sold to Robert King, a Quaker merchant in Montserrat, Equiano was allowed to purchase his own freedom for the sum of forty pounds – no small amount of money at that time – which he raised over three years by skilfully trading goods on his own account. Much of the next twenty years were spent at sea. By the 1780s, Equiano was a well-known public speaker in London who kept the newspapers supplied with a steady stream of letters calling for abolition. His writing attacked slavery apologists like the planters James Tobin and Gordon Turnball, whose own pamphlets attempted to portray slavery as a benign institution.

Equiano also signed and organised several joint letters and petitions issued by 'the Sons of Africa' which were against slavery and represented the views of the Black community in London. The majority of anti-slavery petitions and letters were directed at Parliament, whose members, after all, had the power to change the law. But on 21 March 1788, Equiano took the rather unusual and bold step of writing a personal appeal to Queen Charlotte, wife of George III, even though the monarch himself was known to be hostile to abolition. The letter was duly republished in his autobiography a year later, and the first print run sold out almost immediately. John Wesley, the founder of Methodism, read the book on his deathbed, while one of its first (if not entirely favourable) reviewers was the feminist Mary Wollstonecraft. Equiano issued eight further editions of *The Interesting Narrative* during his lifetime and the book became something of a bible to abolitionists of all creeds. It was rapidly translated into German, Dutch and Russian and was published in the United States.

Equiano died at the age of fifty-two in 1797, ten years before William Wilberforce successfully carried the motion through Parliament to end the slave trade in Britain. A further twenty-six years would elapse before royal assent was given to the Slavery Abolition Act of 1833, which abolished slavery across all of the British colonies and liberated more than 800,000 enslaved people in the Caribbean and South Africa, and some in Canada. Equiano's contribution to abolition is immeasurable; the eloquence with which he was able to recount the horrors of the trade had an enormous effect on helping sway public opinion.

Letter to the Queen:

March the 21st, 1788, I had the honour of presenting the Queen with a petition on behalf of my African brethren, which was received most graciously by her Majesty:

To the QUEEN's most Excellent Majesty.

Madam,

Your Majesty's well known benevolence and humanity emboldens me to approach your royal presence, trusting that the obscurity of my situation will not prevent your Majesty from attending to the sufferings for which I plead. Yet I do not solicit your royal pity for my own distress; my sufferings, although numerous, are in a measure forgotten. I supplicate your Majesty's compassion for millions of my African countrymen, who groan under the lash of tyranny in the West Indies.

The oppression and cruelty exercised to the unhappy negroes there, have at length reached the British legislature, and they are now deliberating on its redress; even several persons of property in slaves in the West Indies, have petitioned parliament against its continuance, sensible that it is as impolitic as it is unjust – and what is inhuman must ever be unwise.

Your Majesty's reign has been hitherto distinguished by private acts of benevolence and bounty; surely the more extended the misery is, the greater claim it has to your Majesty's compassion, and the greater must be your Majesty's pleasure in administering to its relief.

I presume, therefore, gracious Queen, to implore your interposition with your royal consort, in favour of the wretched Africans; that, by your Majesty's benevolent influence, a period may now be put to their misery; and that they may be raised from the condition of brutes, to which they are at present degraded, to the rights and situation of freemen, and admitted to partake of the blessings of your Majesty's happy government; so shall your Majesty enjoy the heartfelt pleasure of procuring happiness to millions, and be rewarded in the grateful prayers of themselves, and of their posterity.

And may the all-bountiful Creator shower on your Majesty, and the Royal Family, every blessing that this world can afford, and every fulness of joy which divine revelation has promised us in the next.

I am your Majesty's most dutiful and devoted servant to command,

Gustavus Vassa,

The Oppressed Ethiopean.

2

Elizabeth Fry's Memorandum on Prisons, 1817

A figurehead of philanthropic endeavour to the late Victorians and posthumously recognised for her benevolent piety, Elizabeth Fry perhaps never forgot that one of her Quaker ancestors had been imprisoned for his religious beliefs in 1682 – the cause which her passionate crusade succeeded in bringing to the world's consciousness was the pitiable state of prisons, and in particular the appalling treatment of women within them. As her biographer June Rose put it, reminding us of her subject's extraordinary radicalism, Fry 'gate-crashed into public life, into an exclusively male preserve, when the idea was unthinkable'.

Her cause was far from fashionable in an age when a girl of nine could be – and in one recorded instance was – sentenced to death for stealing two pennyworths of paints. Court records of the time show that another young woman with a baby just a few weeks old was hanged for stealing a piece of cloth worth a mere five shillings.

Born in Norwich in 1780 to an affluent Quaker banking family, Fry had undertaken various charitable endeavours before she was encouraged by Stephen Grellet, a French-American Quaker, to pay a visit to the women in Newgate Prison in 1814 – he had been appalled by the scenes of degradation he'd witnessed in this most notorious of London's many jails. Fry, having gathered a selection of garments for the women prisoners and their offspring, with some difficulty convinced the governor to allow her and Anna Buxton, a Quaker relative, to enter the women's quarters – as a concession to his fears for their safety, Fry was persuaded to leave her watch behind.

What they found was something akin to Bedlam, with nearly 300 women stuffed into two rooms. They were of all ages, from young girls to frail older women, and dressed in rags – some had been sentenced to death, while others were yet untried. They sat bickering and cursing, those with any money having evidently availed themselves of the prison's liquor tap. The sight that most moved Fry was of two prisoners stripping clothes from a dead baby to clothe a live one.

The death of her own daughter aged only five, among other domestic issues, would mean nearly three years elapsing between Fry's first visits to Newgate and her establishment in April 1817 of a society entitled the Association for the Improvement of the Female Prisoners in Newgate. Less than a year after she began her campaign, a committee of the House of Commons was appointed to examine the conditions of Britain's jails, with Fry called upon to give evidence to it and offer insights into the problem. As a result, improvements were made to the physical conditions. The letter below dates from the run-up to that period, when Fry was in the process of establishing a school for the women in the prison.

Elizabeth Fry Memorandum

4 March 1817

I have just returned from a most melancholy visit to Newgate, where I have been at the request of Elizabeth Fricker [condemned for robbery], previous to her execution to-morrow morning, at eight o'clock. I found her much hurried, distressed, and tormented in mind. Her hands cold, and covered with something like the perspiration preceding death, and in a universal tremor. The women with her, said she had been so outrageous before our going, that they thought a man must be sent for to manage her. However, after a serious time with her, her troubled soul became calmed [. . .]

Besides this poor woman, there are also six men to be hanged, one of whom has a wife near her confinement, also condemned, and six young children. Since the awful report came down, he has become quite mad, from horror of mind. A strait waistcoat could not keep him within bounds: he had just bitten the turnkey; I saw the man come out with his hand bleeding, as I passed the cell. I hear that another, who had been tolerably educated and brought up, was doing all he could to harden himself, through unbelief, trying to convince himself that religious truths were idle tales. In this endeavour he appeared to have been too successful with several of his fellow-sufferers. He sent to beg for a bottle of wine, no doubt in the hope of drowning his misery, and the fears that would arise, by a degree of intoxication. I inquired no further, I had seen and heard enough.

3

Richard Oastler's Letter to the *Leeds Mercury* on Child Labour, 1830

Richard Oastler became steward of the Fixby estate near Huddersfield belonging to Thomas Thornhill, following his father's death in 1820. He was conservative by nature; he saw 'The Altar, The Throne and The Cottage' as the three pillars of British society, and was perturbed by the changes wrought by the Industrial Revolution that had forced labourers off the land into factories and led to traditional crafts being superseded by mechanised mass-production. The pace of the transformation of Britain from a predominantly rural and agrarian country into an urban and industrial one was extraordinarily rapid and entirely unregulated. There were no planning or employment laws. Health and safety regulations were non-existent, and the conditions in the mills and factories that proliferated on once-green fields were often appalling and frequently deadly. There was no limit to the number of hours people could work or to the age of the employees. Accordingly, boys and girls as young as five years of age might toil for up to sixteen hours a day, and were often treated brutally by their overseers. Gruesome and fatal accidents were daily occurrences, with extreme fatigue often the root cause.

This was the issue that Oastler sought to draw attention to when he sent his letter to the editors of the *Leeds Mercury* in 1830. His damning indictment of the factory system, followed by a series of public demonstrations across Yorkshire at which he addressed vast crowds of people, compelled the government to convene a commission to investigate working conditions. As a direct result of his campaign, the first Factory Act was passed in 1833. This new law restricted the length of the working day to eight hours for children under thirteen and to twelve hours for those aged fourteen to eighteen. But Oastler continued to agitate for further improvements to the law and backed a call from mill workers for a ten-hour day for adolescent employees. After many setbacks, including Oastler's three-year imprisonment for debt, the Ten Hours Act was finally passed in 1847.

At a meeting in Bradford, following the Act's official adoption by local employers, an assembly of mill workers placed on record 'their heartfelt gratitude to that noble of nature Richard Oastler, Esq., the originator of, and persevering advocate of the greatest boon to the factory working population in the country'.

SLAVERY IN YORKSHIRE

TO THE EDITORS OF THE LEEDS MERCURY

> "It is the pride of Britain that a slave cannot exist on her soil; and if I read the genius of her constitution aright, I find that Slavery is most abhorrent to it – that the air which Britons breath is free – the ground on which they tread is sacred to liberty."
>
> Rev. R.W. HAMILTON's Speech at the Meeting held in the Cloth-hall Yard, Sept. 22d, 1830

GENTLEMEN, – No heart responded with truer accents to the sounds of liberty which were heard in the Leeds Cloth-hall yard, on the 22d inst. than did mine, and from none could more sincere and earnest prayers arise to the throne of Heaven, that hereafter Slavery might only be known to Britain in the pages of her history. One shade alone obscured my pleasure, arising not from any difference in principle, but from the want of application of the general principle to the whole Empire. The pious and able champions of Negro liberty and Colonial rights should, if I mistake not, have gone farther than they did; or perhaps, to speak more correctly, before they had travelled so far as the West Indies, should, at least for a few moments, have sojourned in our own immediate neighbourhood, and have directed the attention of the meeting to scenes of misery, acts of oppression and victims of slavery, even on the threshold of our homes!

Let truth speak out, appalling as the statements may appear. The fact is true. Thousands of our fellow-creatures and fellow-subjects, both male and female, the miserable inhabitants of a Yorkshire town; (Yorkshire now represented in Parliament by the giant of anti-slavery principles,) are this very moment existing in a state of Slavery more horrid than are victims of that hellish system – "Colonial Slavery." These innocent creatures drawl out unpitied their short but miserable existence, in a place famed for its profession of religious zeal, whose inhabitants are ever foremost in professing "Temperance" and "Reformation," and are striving to outrun their neighbours in Missionary exertions, and would fain send the Bible to the farthest corner of the globe – aye in the very place where the anti-slavery fever rages most furiously, her apparent charity, is not more admired on earth, than her real cruelty is abhorred in heaven. The very streets which receive the droppings of an "Anti-Slavery Society" are every morning wet by the tears of innocent victims at the accursed shrine of avarice, who are compelled (not by the cart-whip of the negro slave-driver) but by the dread of the equally appalling thong or strap of the overlooker, to hasten, half-dressed, but not half-fed, to those magazines of British Infantile Slavery – the Worsted Mills in the town and neighbourhood of Bradford!!!

Would that I had Brougham's eloquence, that I might rouse the hearts of the nation, and make every Briton swear "These innocents shall be free!"

Thousands of little children, both male and female, but principally female, from SEVEN to fourteen years of age, are daily compelled to labour from six o'clock in the morning to seven in the evening, with only – Britons, blush while you read it! – with only thirty minutes allowed for eating and recreation! – Poor infants! ye are indeed sacrificed at the shrine of avarice, without even the solace of the negro slave: – ye are no more than he is, free agents – ye are compelled to work as long as the necessity of your needy parents may require, or the cold-blooded avarice of your worse than barbarian masters may demand! Ye live in the boasted land of freedom, and feel and mourn that ye are Slaves, and slaves without the only comfort which the Negro has. He knows it is his sordid mercenary master's INTEREST that he should live, be strong and healthy. Not so with you. Ye are doomed to labour from morn till night for one who cares not how soon your weak and tender frames are stretched to breaking! You are not mercifully valued at so much per head; this would assure you at least (even with the worst and most cruel masters), of the mercy shown to their own labouring beasts. No, no! your soft and delicate limbs are tired, and fagged, and jaded at only so much per week; and when your joints can act no longer, your emaciated frames are cast aside, the boards on which you lately toiled and wasted life away, are instantly supplied with other victims, who in this boasted land of liberty are HIRED – not sold – as Slaves, and daily forced to hear that they are free. Oh! Duncombe! Thou hatest Slavery – I know thou dost resolve that "Yorkshire children shall no more be slaves." And Morpeth! Who justly gloriest in Christian faith – Oh Morpeth listen to the cries and count the tears of these poor babes and let St. Stephen's hear thee swear – "they shall no longer groan in Slavery!" And Bethell, too! who swears eternal hatred to the name of Slave, whene'er thy manly voice is heard in Britain's senate, assert the rights and liberty of Yorkshire Youths. And Brougham! Thou who art the chosen champion of liberty in every clime! Oh bend thy giant's mind, and listen to the sorrowing accents of these poor Yorkshire little ones, and note their tears; then let thy voice rehearse their woes, and touch the chord thou only holdest – the chord that sounds above the silvery notes in praise of heavenly liberty, and down descending at thy will, groans in the horrid caverns of the deep in muttering sounds of misery accursed to hellish bondage; and as thou soundst these notes, let Yorkshire hear thee swear "Her children shall be free!" Yes, all ye four protectors of our rights, chosen by freemen to destroy oppression's rod,

"Vow one by one, vow altogether, vow
"With heart and voice, eternal enmity
"Against oppression by your brethren's hands;
"Till man nor woman under Britain's laws,
"Nor son nor daughter born within her empire,
"Shall buy or sell, or HIRE, or BE A SLAVE!"

The nation is now most resolutely determined that Negroes shall be free. Let them, however, not forget that Britons have common rights with Afric's sons.

The blacks may be fairly compared to beasts of burden, kept for their master's use. The whites to those which others keep and let for hire! If I have succeeded in calling the attention of your readers to the horrid and abominable system on which the worsted mills in and near Bradford are conducted, I have done some good. Why should not children working in them be protected by legislative enactments, as well as those who work in cotton mills? Christians should feel and act for those whom Christ so eminently loved, and declared that "of such is the kingdom of heaven."

Your insertion of the above in the *Leeds Mercury*, at your earliest convenience, will oblige, Gentlemen,

Your most obedient servant,
RICHARD OASTLER
Fixby-Hall, near Huddersfield, Sept. 29th 1830

4

Karl Marx et al.'s Letter to Abraham Lincoln on his Re-election, 1865

Expelled from his German homeland shortly after the publication of his *Communist Manifesto*, Karl Marx and his family settled permanently in London in 1849. Subsisting on a meagre income from journalism, including a stint as the European correspondent for the *New York Daily Tribune*, Marx frequently wrote in the British Museum's Reading Room and socialised, schemed and generally politicked with fellow émigré radicals in the capital. On 28 September 1864, British, French and German trade union activists gathered at St Martin's Hall near Covent Garden to discuss ways in which greater support might be offered to beleaguered Polish and Italian workers and forge closer co-operation between working people internationally. A new organisation was formed: the International Working Men's Association (IWMA), or the First International. Marx was seemingly only invited at the last minute and, as he later recalled in a letter to his friend Friedrich Engels, merely sat 'in a non-speaking capacity on the platform', but he was not to remain on the sidelines for long. He immediately assumed a central role at IWMA and drafted its opening manifesto, with its battle cry of 'Proletarians of all countries, unite!', and all its subsequent main resolutions.

Marx had been extremely heartened by the fight against slavery in the United States and the part Lancashire mill workers had played in it, by refusing to touch raw cotton picked by slaves, and in preventing Britain from aiding the Confederacy in the American Civil War. Abraham Lincoln himself wrote a letter of thanks in 1863, praising the 'working men of Manchester' for their selfless act of 'sublime Christian heroism'. That same year, Lincoln had issued his Emancipation Proclamation, pronouncing freedom for all slaves in the Confederacy, though slavery would not be officially abolished in America until the passing of the Thirteenth Amendment, after the Civil War's end in 1865.

Minutes from a meeting of the Central (General) Council of the IWMA on 29 November 1864 show that it was Marx who suggested sending a message to the American people 'congratulating them on their having re-elected Abraham Lincoln as President' and subsequently wrote the letter addressed to Lincoln below.

Written by Marx 22–29 November 1864, and first published in the *Bee-Hive Newspaper*, No. 169, 7 January 1865

Sir, –

We congratulate the American people upon your re-election by a large majority. If resistance to the Slave Power was the reserved watchword of your first election, the triumphant war cry of your re-election is Death to Slavery.

From the commencement of the Titanic-American strife the workingmen of Europe felt instinctively that the star-spangled banner carried the destiny of their class. The contest for the territories which opened the dire epopee, was it not to decide whether the virgin soil of immense tracts should be wedded to the labour of the emigrant or prostituted by the tramp of the slavedriver?

When an oligarchy of 300,000 slaveholders dared to inscribe for the first time in the annals of the world "slavery" on the banner of Armed Revolt when on the very spots where hardly a century ago the idea of one great Democratic Republic had first sprung up, whence the first Declaration of the Rights of Man was issued, and the first impulse given to the European revolution of the eighteenth century; when on those very spots counter-revolution, with systematic thoroughness, gloried in rescinding "the ideas entertained at the time of the formation of the old constitution", and maintained slavery to be "a beneficent institution", indeed, the old solution of the great problem of "the relation of capital to labour", and cynically proclaimed property in man "the corner-stone of the new edifice", then the working classes of Europe understood at once, even before the fanatic partisanship of the upper classes for the Confederate gentry had given its dismal warning, that the slaveholders' rebellion was to sound the tocsin for a general holy crusade of property against labour, and that for the men of labour, with their hopes for the future, even their past conquests were at stake in that tremendous conflict on the other side of the Atlantic. Everywhere they bore therefore patiently the hardships imposed upon them by the cotton crisis, opposed enthusiastically the pro-slavery intervention – importunities of their betters – and, from most parts of Europe, contributed their quota of blood to the good cause.

While the working men, the true political powers of the North, allowed slavery to defile their own republic, while before the Negro, mastered and sold without his concurrence, they boasted it the highest prerogative of the white-skinned laborer to sell himself and choose his own master, they were unable to attain the true freedom of labour, or to support their European brethren in their struggle for emancipation; but this barrier to progress has been swept off by the red sea of civil war.

The working men of Europe feel sure that, as the American War of Independence initiated a new era of ascendancy for the middle class, so the American Anti-Slavery War will do for the working classes. They consider it an earnest of the epoch to come that it fell to the lot of Abraham Lincoln, the single-minded son of the working class, to lead his country through the matchless struggle for the rescue of an enchained race and the reconstruction of a social world.

Signed on behalf of the International Working Men's Association, the Central Council:

Longmaid, Worley, Whitlock, Fox, Blackmore, Hartwell, Pidgeon, Lucraft, Weston, Dell, Nieass, Shaw, Lake, Buckley, Osborne, Howell, Carter, Wheeler, Stainsby, Morgan, Grossmith, Dick, Denoual, Jourdain, Morrissot, Leroux, Bordage, Bocquet, Talandier, Dupont, L. Wolff, Aldovrandi, Lama, Solustri, Nusperli, Eccarius, Wolff, Lessner, Pfander, Lochner, Kaub, Bolleter, Rybczinski, Hansen, Schantzenbach, Smales, Cornelius, Petersen, Otto, Bagnagatti, Setacci; George Odger, President of Council; P.V. Lubez, Corresponding Secretary for France; Karl Marx, Corresponding Secretary for Germany; G.P. Fontana, Corresponding Secretary for Italy; J.E. Holtorp, Corresponding Secretary for Poland; H.F. Jung, Corresponding Secretary for Switzerland; William R. Cremer, Honorary General Secretary. 18, Greek Street, Soho.

To be militant in some way or other is, however, a moral obligation. It is a duty which every woman will owe to her own conscience and self-respect, to other women who are less fortunate than herself, and to all those who are to come after her.

Emmeline Pankhurst

5

Barbara Bodichon's Correspondence with Helen Taylor on Women's Suffrage, 1866

The success of the long and arduous campaign for women's suffrage, the basic right to vote on an equal footing with men, rested on the actions of many brave women, a great deal of whose names are well-known and whose heroism is justly celebrated today. Arguably the most prominent remain the remarkable Pankhursts, Emmeline and her daughters Christabel and Sylvia and the indomitable Millicent Fawcett. But while a statue of Fawcett now stands in Parliament Square, few would even recognise the name of the woman who orchestrated the very first petition presented to parliament calling for women's suffrage: Barbara Bodichon.

From a radical Unitarian family and distantly related to Florence Nightingale, Bodichon was a pioneering proto-feminist journalist and co-founder of the *Englishwoman's Review.* Her 1857 pamphlet, *Women and Work*, denounced the legal dependency of wives on their husbands, and throughout her life she continued to campaign for the extension of opportunities for women to study and gain meaningful employment. With the poet and philanthropist Adelaide Anne Procter and the writer Jessie Boucherett, she established the Society for Promoting the Employment of Women in 1859. However, it was their right to vote, or the lack of it, that caused her to put pen to paper. On 9 May 1866, she wrote to Helen Taylor, stepdaughter and secretary to the politician and philosopher John Stuart Mill, mooting the possibility of organising a petition demanding suffrage for women. Taylor gave her backing to the idea, and the petition bearing the signature of 1,499 women was presented by Mill to parliament on their behalf on 7 June 1866. Though unsuccessful, the Fawcett Society is not alone in counting this moment as the start of the organised campaign for votes for women.

---

9 May 1866

My dear Madam,

I am very anxious to have some conversation with you about the possibility of doing something immediately towards getting women votes. I should not like to start a petition or make any movement without knowing what you and Mr J.S. Mill thought expedient at this time. I have only just arrived in London from Algiers but I have already seen many ladies who are willing to take some steps for this cause. Miss BOUCHERETT who is here puts down £25 at once for expenses. I shall be every day this week at this office at 3 here. Could you write a petition – which you could bring with you? I myself should propose to try simply for what we were most likely to get.

yours
Barbara Bodichon

9 May 1866

I think that while a Reform bill is under discussion and petitions are being presented to parliament from various causes – asking for representation or protesting against disfranchisement, it is very desirable that women who wish for political enfranchisement should say and that women [some words scored out – intended to mean 'not'] saying so now will be used against them in the future and delay the time of their enfranchisement . . . this is no reason why women should not ask for what they will never obtain till they have asked for it very long, and I think the most important thing is to make a demand and commence the first humble beginnings of an agitation for which reasons can be given that are in harmony with the political ideals of English people in general. No idea is so universally acceptable in England as that taxation and representation ought to go together, and people in general will be much more willing to the assertion that single women and widows of property have been (unfairly?!) overlooked and left out from privileges to which their property entitles them, than to the much more startling general proposition that sex is not a proper ground for distinction in political rights. It seems to me therefore that a petition asking for the admission to the franchise of all women holding the requisite property qualification would be highly desirable now, quite independently of any immediate results to follow from it. The only doubt is whether enough signatures could be got to prevent it from being insignificant as a demonstration on the part of women themselves. I do not think that less than one hundred would be enough, anything more than that would seem to me very satisfactory. I see no reason why the signatures should be confined to those who would profit by the plan if carried out; it would be perfectly reasonable for all women to ask for the franchise for those among them who can fulfill the conditions at present demanded of all men, just as men who are not £7 householders petition in favour of the present reform bill. We should only be petitioning for the omission of the word *male* or *men* from the present act.

As regards myself I will do my best to preface a sketch of a petition for your consideration but it will take me some days to think over what seem the best heads to put down. Probably the petition finally should be drawn up from the suggestions of many. I am afraid we cannot expect to get many influential names but this would not be of much importance if numbers could be got.

If a tolerably numerously signed petition can be got up my father will gladly undertake to present it and will consider whether it might be made the occasion for anything further. He could at least move for the return of the number of householders disqualified on account of sex, which could be useful to us in many ways if it could be got.

I shall be very glad to subscribe £20 towards expenses and may perhaps be able to call at 19 Langham Place on Friday or Saturday at the time you mention.

Helen Taylor

6

Colonel Robert Loyd-Lindsay's Letter to *The Times* on War, 1870

On learning of his death in 1901, Florence Nightingale, 'The Lady with the Lamp', wrote: 'Lord Wantage is a great loss but he had been a great gain. And what he has gained for us can never be lost. It is my experience that such men exist only in England. A man who had everything (to use the common phrase), but who worked as hard, and to the last, as the poorest able man – and all for others – for the common good.'

Colonel Robert Loyd-Lindsay, 1st Baron Wantage, was a soldier with a highly distinguished military career, who had earned the Victoria Cross for valour for his actions in the Battles of the Alma and Inkerman during the Crimean War. Like Nightingale, Wantage, who had nearly died of dysentery, had been appalled by the suffering endured by soldiers in the field. His indignant letters home laid bare how the poor conditions had been exacerbated by the bungled logistics of incompetent and out-of-touch British military top brass. It was out of concern for ordinary servicemen at the outbreak of the Franco-Prussian War in 1870 (a conflict in which Britain had allies on both sides) that he wrote to *The Times*, proposing the creation of a neutral, impartial aid organisation to help wounded soldiers from either army.

In the wake of the letter, various philanthropists convened on 4 August 1870 and a resolution was passed to create the National Society for Aid to the Sick and Wounded in War, the organisation that, in 1905, became the British Red Cross. Its express purpose was to give aid 'impartially to the sick and wounded of the belligerent armies'; meanwhile it would 'not attempt to interfere with state operations, or military medical staff, but only to help them in relieving the miseries of war'.

Loyd-Lindsay would serve as its first chairman and his wife, amanuensis, constant companion and philanthropist in her own right, Harriet, headed up the women's committee.

---

22 July 1870

The news which daily reaches us from abroad shows that nations can at times go mad as well as individuals. It is strange to read in your columns of the preparations which are being made simultaneously to destroy life and to save it. Unfortunately it is far easier to destroy than to save, all the glory being reserved for the former, and ten times the scientific resources being devoted to it.

The part that we [the British] may be destined to take in this war is unknown, but we know well that as soon as a battle has been fought there will be a large amount of sympathy excited on behalf of the wounded soldiers on both sides for the French, our staunch and faithful allies in the Crimea, with whom I, in common with many others, spent two years in constant and friendly intercourse, and for the Prussians, related to us by ties of friendship, and by our Princess Royal, destined to be their Queen.

The difficulty will be how properly to direct our friendly aid. England has before now marked her sympathy in various wars by largely contributing aid and succour to the wounded on one side but any one-sided demonstration would in this case be singularly out of place. What is done, should be done impartially and, above all, systematically.

7

George Washington Williams' Letter to King Leopold II of Belgium on the Congo, 1890

Buried, somewhat surprisingly, in Blackpool's Layton Cemetery in Lancashire, George Washington Williams was an African-American journalist, a Civil War veteran and the first black member of the Ohio General Assembly. He was also among the earliest people to publicise the diabolical horrors of King Leopold II of Belgium in Congo Free State.

Williams, who penned the vast two-volume *History of the Negro Race in America from 1619 to 1880*, the first survey of the African-American experience to be written and published by a member of that community, subsequently both won an audience with King Leopold in Belgium and obtained a commission from a press agency to write a series of articles about this emerging African state. Initially enthusiastic about what he naively assumed might be a nation free of prejudice, one whose autocratic ruler blithely maintained it had been established out of purely 'Christian duty to the poor African', Williams was to encounter exploitation on an almost industrial scale on his visit there in 1890. His damning open letter to King Leopold was published in newspapers around the world and shone a light on the truly unconscionable face of European colonialism.

An Open Letter to His Serene Majesty Leopold II, King of the Belgians and Sovereign of the Independent State of Congo by Colonel, The Honorable George W. Williams, of the United States of America

Good and Great Friend,

I have the honour to submit for your Majesty's consideration some reflections respecting the Independent State of Congo, based upon a careful study and inspection of the country and character of the personal Government you have established upon the African Continent.

It afforded me great pleasure to avail myself of the opportunity afforded me last year, of visiting your State in Africa; and how thoroughly I have been disenchanted, disappointed and disheartened, it is now my painful duty to make known to your Majesty in plain but respectful language. Every charge which I am about to bring against your Majesty's personal Government in the Congo has been carefully investigated; a list of competent and veracious witnesses, documents, letters, official records and data has been faithfully prepared, which will be deposited with Her Britannic Majesty's Secretary of State for Foreign Affairs, until such time as an International Commission can be created with power to send for persons and papers, to administer oaths, and attest the truth or falsity of these charges.

There were instances in which Mr HENRY M. STANLEY sent one white man, with four or five Zanzibar soldiers, to make treaties with native chiefs. The staple argument was that the white man's heart had grown sick of the wars and rumours of war between one chief and another, between one village and another; that the white man was at peace with his black brother, and desired to "confederate all African tribes" for the general defense and public welfare. All the sleight-of-hand tricks had been carefully rehearsed, and he was now ready for his work. A number of electric batteries had been purchased in London, and when attached to the arm under the coat, communicated with a band of ribbon which passed over the palm of the white brother's hand, and when he gave the black brother a cordial grasp of the hand the black brother was greatly surprised to find his white brother so strong, that he nearly knocked him off his feet in giving him the hand of fellowship. When the native inquired about the disparity of strength between himself and his white brother, he was told that the white man could pull up trees and perform the most prodigious feats of strength. Next came the lens act. The white brother took from his pocket a cigar, carelessly bit off the end, held up his glass to the sun and complaisantly smoked his cigar to the great amazement and terror of his black brother. The white man explained his intimate relation to the sun, and declared that if he were to request him to burn up his black brother's village it would be done. The third act was the gun trick. The white man took a percussion cap gun, tore the end of the paper which held the powder to the bullet, and poured the powder and paper into the gun, at the same time slipping the bullet into the sleeve of the left arm. A cap was placed upon the nipple of the gun, and the black brother was implored to step off ten yards and shoot at his white brother to demonstrate his statement that he was a spirit, and, therefore, could not be killed. After much begging the black brother aims the gun at his white brother, pulls the trigger, the gun is discharged, the white man stoops . . . and takes the bullet from his shoe!

By such means as these, too silly and disgusting to mention, and a few boxes of gin, whole villages have been signed away to your Majesty.

When I arrived in the Congo, I naturally sought for the results of the brilliant programme: "fostering care", "benevolent enterprise", an "honest and practical effort" to increase the knowledge of the natives "and secure their welfare". I had never been able to conceive of Europeans, establishing a government in a tropical country, without building a hospital; and yet from the mouth of the Congo River to its head-waters, here at the seventh cataract, a distance of 1,448 miles, there is not a solitary hospital for Europeans, and only three sheds for sick Africans in the service of the State, not fit to be occupied by a horse. Sick sailors frequently die on board their vessels at Banana Point; and if it were not for the humanity of the Dutch Trading Company at that place – who have often opened their private hospital to the sick of other countries – many more might die. There is not a single chaplain in the employ of your Majesty's Government to console the sick or bury the dead. Your white men sicken and die in their quarters or on the caravan road, and seldom have Christian burial. With few exceptions, the surgeons of your Majesty's Government have been gentlemen of professional ability, devoted to duty, but usually left with few medical stores and no quarters in which to treat their patients. The African soldiers and labourers of your Majesty's Government fare worse than the whites, because they have poorer quarters, quite as bad as those of the natives; and in the sheds, called hospitals, they languish upon a bed of bamboo poles without blankets, pillows or any food different from that served to them when well, rice and fish.

I was anxious to see to what extent the natives had "adopted the fostering care" of your Majesty's "benevolent enterprise", and I was doomed to bitter disappointment. Instead of the natives of the Congo "adopting the fostering care" of your Majesty's Government, they everywhere complain that their land has been taken from them by force; that the Government is cruel and arbitrary, and declare that they neither love nor respect the Government and its flag. Your Majesty's Government has sequestered their land, burned their towns, stolen their property, enslaved their women and children, and committed other crimes too numerous to mention in detail. It is natural that they everywhere shrink from "the fostering care" your Majesty's Government so eagerly proffers them. There has been, to my absolute knowledge, no "honest and practical effort made to increase their knowledge and secure their welfare." Your Majesty's Government has never spent one franc for educational purposes, nor instituted any practical system of industrialism. Indeed the most unpractical measures have been adopted against the natives in nearly every respect; and in the capital of your Majesty's Government at Boma there is not a native employed. The labour system is radically unpractical; the soldiers and labourers of your Majesty's Government are very largely imported from Zanzibar at a cost of £10 per capita, and from Sierra Leone, Liberia, Accra and Lagos at from £1 to £1/10 per capita. These recruits are transported under circumstances more cruel than cattle in European countries. They eat their rice twice a day by the use of their fingers; they often thirst for water when the season is dry; they are exposed to the heat and rain, and sleep upon the damp and filthy decks of the vessels often so closely crowded as to lie in human ordure. And, of course, many die.

Upon the arrival of the survivors in the Congo they are set to work as labourers at one shilling a day; as soldiers they are promised sixteen shillings per month, in English money, but are usually paid off in cheap handkerchiefs and poisonous gin. The cruel and unjust treatment to which these people are subjected breaks the spirits of many of them, makes them distrust and despise your Majesty's Government. They are enemies, not patriots.

There are from sixty to seventy officers of the Belgian army in the service of your Majesty's Government in the Congo of whom only about thirty are at their post; the other half are in Belgium on furlough. These officers draw double pay – as soldiers and as civilians. It is not my duty to criticise the unlawful and unconstitutional use of these officers coming into the service of this African State. Such criticism will come with more grace from some Belgian statesman, who may remember that there is no constitutional or organic relation subsisting between his Government and the purely personal and absolute monarchy your Majesty has established in Africa. But I take the liberty to say that many of these officers are too young and inexperienced to be entrusted with the difficult work of dealing with native races. They are ignorant of native character, lack wisdom, justice, fortitude and patience. They have estranged the natives from your Majesty's Government, have sown the seed of discord between tribes and villages, and some of them have stained the uniform of the Belgian officer with murder, arson and robbery. Other officers have served the State faithfully, and deserve well of their Royal Master.

From these general observations I wish now to pass to specific charges against your Majesty's Government.

FIRST.—Your Majesty's Government is deficient in the moral military and financial strength, necessary to govern a territory of

1,508,000 square miles, 7,251 miles of navigation, and 31,694 square miles of lake surface. In the Lower Congo River there is but one post, in the cataract region one. From Leopoldville to N'Gombe, a distance of more than 300 miles, there is not a single soldier or civilian. Not one out of every twenty State-officials know the language of the natives, although they are constantly issuing laws, difficult even for Europeans, and expect the natives to comprehend and obey them. Cruelties of the most astounding character are practised by the natives, such as burying slaves alive in the grave of a dead chief, cutting off the heads of captured warriors in native combats, and no effort is put forth by your Majesty's Government to prevent them. Between 800 and 1,000 slaves are sold to be eaten by the natives of the Congo State annually; and slave raids, accomplished by the most cruel and murderous agencies, are carried on within the territorial limits of your Majesty's Government which is impotent. There are only 2,300 soldiers in the Congo.

SECOND.—Your Majesty's Government has established nearly fifty posts, consisting of from two to eight mercenary slave-soldiers from the East Coast. There is no white commissioned officer at these posts; they are in charge of the black Zanzibar soldiers, and the State expects them not only to sustain themselves, but to raid enough to feed the garrisons where the white men are stationed. These piratical, buccaneering posts compel the natives to furnish them with fish, goats, fowls, and vegetables at the mouths of their muskets; and whenever the natives refuse to feed these vampires, they report to the main station and white officers come with an expeditionary force and burn away the homes of the natives. These black soldiers, many of whom are slaves, exercise the power of life and death. They are ignorant and cruel, because they do not comprehend the natives; they are imposed upon them by the State. They make no report as to the number of robberies they commit, or the number of lives they take; they are only required to subsist upon the natives and thus relieve your Majesty's Government of the cost of feeding them. They are the greatest curse the country suffers now.

THIRD.—Your Majesty's Government is guilty of violating its contracts made with its soldiers, mechanics and workmen, many of whom are subjects of other Governments. Their letters never reach home.

FOURTH.—The Courts of your Majesty's Government are abortive, unjust, partial and delinquent. I have personally witnessed and examined their clumsy operations. The laws printed and circulated in Europe "for the Protection of the blacks" in the Congo, are a dead letter and a fraud. I have heard an officer of the Belgian Army pleading the cause of a white man of low degree who had been guilty of beating and stabbing a black man, and urging race distinctions and prejudices as good and sufficient reasons why his client should be adjudged innocent. I know of prisoners remaining in custody for six and ten months because they were not judged. I saw the white servant of the Governor-General, CAMILLE JANSSEN, detected in stealing a bottle of wine from a hotel table. A few hours later the Procurer-General searched his room and found many more stolen bottles of wine and other things, not the property of servants. No one can be prosecuted in the State of Congo without an order of the Governor-General, and as he refused to allow his servant to be arrested, nothing could be done. The black servants in the hotel, where the wine had been stolen, had been often accused and beaten for these thefts, and now they were glad to be vindicated. But to the surprise of every honest man, the thief was sheltered by the Governor General of your Majesty's Government.

FIFTH—Your Majesty's Government is excessively cruel to its prisoners, condemning them, for the slightest offences, to the chain gang, the like of which can not be seen in any other Government in the civilized or uncivilized world. Often these ox-chains eat into the necks of the prisoners and produce sores about which the flies circle, aggravating the running wound; so the prisoner is constantly worried. These poor creatures are frequently beaten with a dried piece of hippopotamus skin, called a "chicote", and usually the blood flows at every stroke when well laid on. But the cruelties visited upon soldiers and workmen are not to be compared with the sufferings of the poor natives who, upon the slightest pretext, are thrust into the wretched prisons here in the Upper River. I cannot deal with the dimensions of these prisons in this letter, but will do so in my report to my Government.

SIXTH.—Women are imported into your Majesty's Government for immoral purposes. They are introduced by two methods, viz., black men are dispatched to the Portuguese coast where they engage these women as mistresses of white men, who pay to the procurer a monthly sum. The other method is by capturing native women and condemning them to seven years' servitude for some imaginary crime against the State with which the villages of these women are charged. The State then hires these women out to the highest bidder, the officers having the first choice and then the men. Whenever children are born of such relations, the State maintains that the women being its property the child belongs to it also. Not long ago a Belgian trader had a child by a slave-woman of the State, and he tried to secure possession of it that he might educate it, but the Chief of the Station where he resided, refused to be moved by his entreaties. At length he appealed to the Governor-General, and he gave him the woman and thus the trader obtained the child also. This was, however, an unusual case of generosity and clemency; and there is only one post that I know of where there is not to be found children of the civil and military officers of your Majesty's Government abandoned to degradation; white men bringing their own flesh and blood under the lash of a most cruel master, the State of Congo.

SEVENTH.—Your Majesty's Government is engaged in trade and commerce, competing with the organised trade companies of Belgium, England, France, Portugal and Holland. It taxes all trading companies and exempts its own goods from export-duty, and makes many of its officers ivory-traders, with the promise of a liberal commission upon all they can buy or get for the State. State soldiers patrol many villages forbidding the natives to trade with any person but a State official, and when the natives refuse to accept the price of the State, their goods are seized by the

Government that promised them "protection". When natives have persisted in trading with the trade-companies the State has punished their independence by burning the villages in the vicinity of the trading houses and driving the natives away.

EIGHTH.—Your Majesty's Government has violated the General Act of the Conference of Berlin by firing upon native canoes; by confiscating the property of natives; by intimidating native traders, and preventing them from trading with white trading companies; by quartering troops in native villages when there is no war; by causing vessels bound from "Stanley-Pool" to "Stanley-Falls", to break their journey and leave the Congo, ascend the Aruhwimi river to Basoko, to be visited and show their papers; by forbidding a mission steamer to fly its national flag without permission from a local Government; by permitting the natives to carry on the slave-trade, and by engaging in the wholesale and retail slave-trade itself.

NINTH.—-Your Majesty's Government has been, and is now, guilty of waging unjust and cruel wars against natives, with the hope of securing slaves and women, to minister to the behests of the officers of your Government. In such slave-hunting raids one village is armed by the State against the other, and the force thus secured is incorporated with the regular troops. I have no adequate terms with which to depict to your Majesty the brutal acts of your soldiers upon such raids as these. The soldiers who open the combat are usually the bloodthirsty cannibalistic Bangalas, who give no quarter to the aged grandmother or nursing child at the breast of its mother. There are instances in which they have brought the heads of their victims to their white officers on the expeditionary steamers, and afterwards eaten the bodies of slain children. In one war two Belgian Army officers saw, from the deck of their steamer, a native in a canoe some distance away. He was not a combatant and was ignorant of the conflict in progress upon the shore, some distance away. The officers made a wager of £5 that they could hit the native with their rifles. Three shots were fired and the native fell dead, pierced through the head, and the trade canoe was transformed into a funeral barge and floated silently down the river.

TENTH.—Your Majesty's Government is engaged in the slave-trade, wholesale and retail. It buys and sells and steals slaves. Your Majesty's Government gives £3 per head for ablebodied slaves for military service. Officers at the chief stations get the men and receive the money when they are transferred to the State; but there are some middle-men who only get from twenty to twenty-five francs per head. Three hundred and sixteen slaves were sent down the river recently, and others are to follow. These poor natives are sent hundreds of miles away from their villages, to serve among other natives whose language they do not know. When these men run away a reward of 1,000 N'taka is offered. Not long ago such a recaptured slave was given one hundred "chikote" each day until he died. Three hundred N'taka – brassrod – is the price the State pays for a slave, when bought from a native. The labour force at the stations of your Majesty's Government in the Upper River is composed of slaves of all ages and both sexes.

ELEVENTH.—Your Majesty's Government has concluded a contract with the Arab Governor at this place for the establishment of a line of military posts from the Seventh Cataract to Lake Tanganyika territory to which your Majesty has no more legal claim, than I have to be Commander-in-Chief of the Belgian army. For this work the Arab Governor is to receive five hundred stands of arms, five thousand kegs of powder, and £20,000 sterling, to be paid in several instalments. As I write, the news reaches me that these much-treasured and long-looked for materials of war are to be discharged at Basoko, and the Resident here is to be given the discretion as to the distribution of them. There is a feeling of deep discontent among the Arabs here, and they seem to feel that they are being trifled with. As to the significance of this move Europe and America can judge without any comment from me, especially England.

TWELFTH—The agents of your Majesty's Government have misrepresented the Congo country and the Congo railway. Mr. H.M. STANLEY, the man who was your chief agent in setting up your authority in this country, has grossly misrepresented the character of the country. Instead of it being fertile and productive it is sterile and unproductive. The natives can scarcely subsist upon the vegetable life produced in some parts of the country. Nor will this condition of affairs change until the native shall have been taught by the European the dignity, utility and blessing of labour. There is no improvement among the natives, because there is an impassable gulf between them and your Majesty's Government, a gulf which can never be bridged. HENRY M. STANLEY'S name produces a shudder among this simple folk when mentioned; they remember his broken promises, his copious profanity, his hot temper, his heavy blows, his severe and rigorous measures, by which they were mulcted of their lands. His last appearance in the Congo produced a profound sensation among them, when he led 500 Zanzibar soldiers with 300 camp followers on his way to relieve EMIN PASHA. They thought it meant complete subjugation, and they fled in confusion. But the only thing they found in the wake of his march was misery. No white man commanded his rear column, and his troops were allowed to straggle, sicken and die; and their bones were scattered over more than two hundred miles of territory.

CONCLUSIONS

Against the deceit, fraud, robberies, arson, murder, slave-raiding, and general policy of cruelty of your Majesty's Government to the natives, stands their record of unexampled patience, long-suffering and forgiving spirit, which put the boasted civilisation and professed religion of your Majesty's Government to the blush. During thirteen years only one white man has lost his life by the hands of the natives, and only two white men have been killed in the Congo. Major Barttelot was shot by a Zanzibar soldier, and the captain of a Belgian trading-boat was the victim of his own rash and unjust treatment of a native chief.

All the crimes perpetrated in the Congo have been done in your name, and you must answer at the bar of Public Sentiment for the misgovernment of a people, whose lives and fortunes were entrusted to you by the august Conference of Berlin, 1884–1885. I now appeal to the Powers which committed this infant State to your Majesty's charge, and to the great States which gave it international being; and whose majestic law you have scorned and trampled upon, to call and create an International Commission to investigate the charges herein preferred in the name of Humanity, Commerce, Constitutional Government and Christian Civilisation.

I base this appeal upon the terms of Article 36 of Chapter VII of the General Act of the Conference of Berlin, in which that august assembly of Sovereign States reserved to themselves the right "to introduce into it later and by common accord the modifications or ameliorations, the utility of which may be demonstrated experience".

I appeal to the Belgian people and to their Constitutional Government, so proud of its traditions, replete with the song and story of its champions of human liberty, and so jealous of its present position in the sisterhood of European States – to cleanse itself from the imputation of the crimes with which your Majesty's personal State of Congo is polluted.

I appeal to Anti-Slavery Societies in all parts of Christendom, to Philanthropists, Christians, Statesmen, and to the great mass of people everywhere, to call upon the Governments of Europe, to hasten the close of the tragedy your Majesty's unlimited Monarchy is enacting in the Congo.

I appeal to our Heavenly Father, whose service is perfect love, in witness of the purity of my motives and the integrity of my aims; and to history and mankind I appeal for the demonstration and vindication of the truthfulness of the charge I have herein briefly outlined.

And all this upon the word of honour of a gentleman, I subscribe myself your Majesty's humble and obedient servant,

GEORGE W. WILLIAMS
Stanley Falls, Central Africa

18 July 1890

8

Leo Tolstoy's Letter to Mahatma Gandhi on Passive Resistance, 1910

Towards the end of his long life, the great Russian novelist and thinker Leo Tolstoy entered into a correspondence with Mahatma Gandhi. Gandhi was then living in South Africa, where he had gone to practise law in 1893, at the age of twenty-four. A nervous young lawyer on his arrival, his experience of the injustice of British rule there turned him into a campaigner and journalist, and caused him to put his legal skills to use, securing rights for the minority Indian population in South Africa. He also developed some of the methods of non-violent protest that he would subsequently employ in the battle to secure independence for his native India. In 1908, the author of *War and Peace* and *Anna Karenina* had written a letter in support of Indian independence that appeared in the Indian newspaper *Free Hindustan*. Gandhi requested permission to republish it in his own South African paper, *Indian Opinion*, thereby starting an exchange of letters that would last until Tolstoy's death at the age of eighty-two, in November 1910.

In this letter, written when the author had less than three months to live, Tolstoy discusses Gandhi's ideas of using passive resistance to bring about positive change and outlines his own belief in these ideas' broader benefits to humanity as a whole.

To Gandhi, Johannesburg, Transvaal, South Africa

KOCHETY. 7th September 1910.

I received your journal, *Indian Opinion*, and was glad to see what it says of those who renounce all resistance by force, and I immediately felt a wish to let you know what thoughts its perusal aroused in me.

The longer I live – especially now when I clearly feel the approach of death – the more I feel moved to express what I feel more strongly than anything else, and what in my opinion is of immense importance, namely, what we call the renunciation of all opposition by force, which really simply means the doctrine of the law of love unperverted by sophistries. Love, or in other words the striving of men's souls towards unity and the submissive behaviour to one another that results therefrom, represents the highest and indeed the only law of life, as every man knows and feels in the depths of his heart (and as we see most clearly in children), and knows until he becomes involved in the lying net of worldly thoughts. This law was announced by all the philosophies – Indian as well as Chinese, and Jewish, Greek and Roman. Most clearly, I think, was it announced by Christ, who said explicitly that on it hang all the Law and the Prophets. More than that, foreseeing the distortion that has hindered its recognition and may always hinder it, he specially indicated the danger of a misrepresentation that presents itself to men living by worldly interests – namely, that they may claim a right to defend their interests by force or, as he expressed it, to repay blow by blow and recover stolen property by force, etc., etc. He knew, as all reasonable men must do, that any employment of force is incompatible with love as the highest law of life, and that as soon as the use of force appears permissible even in a single case, the law itself is immediately negatived. The whole of Christian civilization, outwardly so splendid, has grown up on this strange and flagrant – partly intentional but chiefly unconscious – misunderstanding and contradiction. At bottom, however, the law of love is, and can be, no longer valid if defence by force is set up beside it. And if once the law of love is not valid, then there remains no law except the right of might. In that state Christendom has lived for 1,900 years. Certainly men have always let themselves be guided by force as the main principle of their social order. The difference between the Christian and all other nations is only this: that in Christianity the law of love had been more clearly and definitely given than in any other religion, and that its adherents solemnly recognized it. Yet despite this they deemed the use of force to be permissible, and based their lives on violence – so that the life of the

Christian nations presents a greater contradiction between what they believe and the principle on which their lives are built: a contradiction between love which should prescribe the law of conduct, and the employment of force, recognized under various forms – such as governments, courts of justice, and armies, which are accepted as necessary and esteemed. This contradiction increased with the development of the spiritual life of Christianity and in recent years has reached the utmost tension.

The question now is, that we must choose one of two things – either to admit that we recognize no religious ethics at all but let our conduct of life be decided by the right of might; or to demand that all compulsory levying of taxes be discontinued, and all our legal and police institutions, and above all, military institutions, be abolished.

This spring, at a scripture examination in a Moscow girls' school, first their religious teacher and then an archbishop who was also present, questioned the girls on the ten commandments, especially on the sixth. After the commandments had been correctly recited the archbishop sometimes put a question, usually: 'Is it always and in every case forbidden by the law of God to kill?' And the unfortunate girls, misled by their instructor, had to answer and did answer: 'Not always, for it is permissible in war and at executions.' When, however, this customary additional question – whether it is always a sin to kill – was put to one of these unfortunate creatures (what I am telling you is not an anecdote, but actually happened and was told me by an eyewitness) the girl coloured up and answered decidedly and with emotion – 'Always!' And despite all the customary sophistries of the archbishop, she held steadfastly to it – that to kill is under all circumstances forbidden even in the Old Testament, and that Christ has not only forbidden us to kill, but in general to do any harm to our neighbour. The archbishop, for all his majesty and verbal dexterity, was silenced, and victory remained with the girl.

Yes, we may write in the papers of our progress in mastery of the air, of complicated diplomatic relations, of various clubs, of discoveries, of all sorts of alliances, and of so-called works of art, and we can pass lightly over what that girl said. But we cannot completely silence her, for every Christian feels the same, however vaguely he may do so. Socialism, Communism, Anarchism, Salvation Armies, the growth of crime, freedom from toil, the increasingly absurd luxury of the rich and increased misery of the poor, the fearfully rising number of suicides – are all indications of that inner contradiction which must and will be resolved. And, of course, resolved in such a manner that the law of love will be recognized and all reliance on force abandoned. Your work in the Transvaal, which to us seems to be at the end of the earth, is yet in the centre of our interest and supplies the most weighty practical proof, in which the world can now share, and not only the Christian but all the peoples of the world can participate.

I think it will please you to hear that here in Russia, too, a similar movement is rapidly attracting attention, and refusals of military service increase year by year. However small as yet is with you the number of those who renounce all resistance by force, and with us the number of men who refuse any military service – both the one and the other can say: God is with us, and God is mightier than man.

In the confession of Christianity – even a Christianity deformed as is that taught among us – and a simultaneous belief in the necessity of armies and preparations to slaughter on an ever-increasing scale, there is an obvious contradiction that cries to heaven, and that sooner or later, but probably quite soon, must appear in the light of day in its complete nakedness. That, however, will either annihilate the Christian religion, which is indispensable for the maintenance of the State, or it will sweep away the military and all the use of force bound up with it – which the State needs no less. All governments are aware of this contradiction, your British as much as our Russian, and therefore its recognition will be more energetically opposed by the governments than any other activity inimical to the State, as we in Russia have experienced and as is shown by the articles in your magazine. The governments know from what direction the greatest danger threatens them, and are on guard with watchful eyes not merely to preserve their interests but actually to fight for their very existence.

Yours etc.,
LEO TOLSTOY

9

Emmeline Pankhurst's Letter on Suffragette Militancy, 1913

If Barbara Bodichon's petition in 1866 ultimately proved a failure, the cause of women's suffrage would only grow in importance, becoming one of the biggest political issues in Britain during the early years of the twentieth century. Its prominence was increased by the decision of some women to adopt a militant stance in favour of direct action to achieve their goals. The fight for votes for women had previously been led by the far more peaceable National Union of Women's Suffrage Societies (NUWSS), headed by Millicent Fawcett since its formation in 1897. Fawcett and her supporters, who called themselves suffragists, believed for the most part that women would only win the vote if they made their case rationally and in a reasonable, legal manner, via petitions, temperate public events and posters and leaflets. But others, particularly Emmeline Pankhurst, were frustrated by the lack of progress and held that a more radical approach was necessary. Pankhurst had founded the Women's Social and Political Union (WSPU) in Manchester in 1903, with her daughters Christabel and Sylvia. These suffragettes, as they had become known, started to publicise their cause by smashing windows, chaining themselves to railings, attacking anti-suffrage MPs with umbrellas and handbags, and even conducting arson attacks on disobliging politicians' carriages, cars and homes. On two occasions, militants even managed to assault the Liberal Prime Minister Herbert Asquith, whose long-held and unwavering opposition to women's suffrage put him at odds with the majority of his own party but ensured that several promising attempts to change the law were scuppered.

Such lawless guerrilla tactics alienated some women but excited and inspired others. There was no shortage of risk of injury, arrest or imprisonment, but many heeded such calls as the one below by

Pankhurst to stay the course until the vote was won. Arguably, these radical acts were also about breaking free of the existing and stifling conventions that dictated what was seemly for women.

As one radical. Mary Richardson, recalled, years later:

> Our suffragette campaign was for much more than 'Votes for Women'. We were women in revolt, led and financed by women. We inaugurated a new era for women and demonstrated for the first time in history that women were capable of fighting their battles for freedom's sake. We were breaking down old senseless barriers which were the curse of our sex, exploding men's theories and ideas about us.

Mrs Pankhurst, Hon. Treasurer, Mrs Mabel Tuke, Hon. Secretary

All communications, unless marked 'private' will be opened by the Hon. Secretary

Private and Confidential

VOTES FOR WOMEN
The Women's Social and Political Union
OFFICE: LINCOLN'S INN HOUSE, KINGSWAY, W.C.
Auditors: Messrs. Sayers & Wesson
Chartered Accountants, 19 Hanover Square, W.
Telegraphic Address – WOSPOLU, LONDON
Telephone 2724 Holborn (three lines)

January 10th, 1913.

Dear Friend,

The Prime Minister has announced that in the week beginning January 20th the Women's Amendments to the Manhood Suffrage Bill will be discussed and voted upon. This means that within a few short days the fate of these Amendments will be finally decided.

The W.S.P.U. has from the first declined to call any truce on the strength of the Prime Minister's so-called pledge, and has refused to depend upon the Amendments in question, because the Government have not accepted the responsibility of getting them carried. There are, however, some Suffragists – and there may be some even in the ranks of the W.S.P.U. – who hope against hope that in spite of the Government's intrigues an unofficial Amdendment may be carried. Feeling as they do, these Suffragists are tempted to hold their hand as far as militancy is concerned, until after the fate of the Amendments is known.

But every member of the W.S.P.U. recognises that the defeat of these Amendments will make militancy more a moral duty and more a political necessity than it has ever been before. We must prepare beforehand to deal with that situation!

There are degrees of militancy. Some women are able to go further than others in militant action and each woman is the judge of her own duty so far as that is concerned. To be militant in some way or other is, however, a moral obligation. It is a duty which every woman will owe to her own conscience and self-respect, to other women who are less fortunate than herself, and to all those who are to come after her.

If any woman refrains from militant protest against the injury done by the Government and the House of Commons to women and to the race, she will share the responsibility for the crime. Submission under such circumstances will be itself a crime.

I know that the defeat of the Amendments will prove to thousands of women that to rely only on peaceful, patient methods, is to court failure, and that militancy is inevitable.

We must, as I have said, prepare to meet the crisis before it arises. Will you therefore tell me (by letter, if it is not possible to do so by word of mouth), that you are ready to take your share in manifesting in a practical manner your indignation at the betrayal of our cause.

Yours sincerely,
E. Pankhurst

When a law has outgrown time and necessity, it must go and the only way to get rid of the law, is to awaken the public to the fact that it has outlived its purposes and that is precisely what I have been doing and mean to do in the future.

Emma Goldman

10

Emily Hobhouse et al.'s Open Letter to the Women of Germany and Austria, 1914

Emily Hobhouse was the youngest daughter of a staunchly conservative Cornish archdeacon. Upon his death in 1895, Hobhouse dedicated herself to welfare work, spending some time in Minnesota where she attended to the families of impoverished Cornish miners who had emigrated to America. At the onset of the Second Boer War she travelled to South Africa to provide relief, and on her return to Britain began speaking out about the poor conditions of the concentration camps into which displaced South African women and children were being herded by the British. Her testimony, though resented by the government, led to the establishment of a Ladies' Commission overseen by Millicent Fawcett to investigate and then instigate any necessary improvements of conditions at the camps. Fawcett was also the president of the National Union of Women's Suffrage Societies, the moderate suffragists' wing of the campaign for votes for women. Or, more accurately, votes for women who were over thirty and owned property. Hobhouse, meanwhile, had served as the Chair of the People's Suffrage Federation, an organisation calling for the more radical universal vote for all. With the outbreak of the First World War, both Fawcett and the militant suffragette leaders Emmeline and Christabel Pankhurst called upon their followers to abandon their protests and put their energy into supporting the war effort. However, Emily Hobhouse, along with Sylvia Pankhurst, was among those suffrage campaigners who fervently opposed the war and refused to toe the party line.

Hobhouse would go on to join the Women's International League for Peace and Freedom, tour occupied Belgium and meet the German Foreign Secretary, Gottlieb von Jagow, in Berlin as part of her personal mission to secure a peaceful resolution to the war. Her major opening salvo in this campaign, though, was an open letter to the women of Germany and Austria that she drafted in December 1914, and which was subsequently signed by a hundred women.

To The WOMEN OF GERMANY AND AUSTRIA.
Open Christmas Letter from Manchester Suffragettes

SISTERS,

Some of us wish to send you a word at this sad Christmastide though we can but speak through the press. The Christmas message sounds like mockery to a world at war, but those of us who wished and still wish for peace may surely offer a solemn greeting to such of you who feel as we do. Do not let us forget that our very anguish unites us, that we are passing together through the same experience of pain and grief.

Caught in the grip of terrible Circumstance, what can we do? Tossed on this turbulent sea of human conflict, we can but moor ourselves to those calm shores whereon stand, like rocks, the eternal verities – Love, Peace, Brotherhood.

We pray you to believe that come what may we hold to our faith in Peace and Goodwill between nations; while technically at emnity in obedience to our rulers, we own allegiance to that higher law which bids us live at peace with all men.

Though our sons are sent to slay each other, and our hearts are torn by the cruelty of this fate, yet through pain supreme we will be true to our common womanhood. We will let no bitterness enter into this tragedy, made sacred by the life-blood of our best, nor mar with hate the heroism of their sacrifice. Though much has been done on all sides you will, as deeply as ourselves, deplore, shall we not steadily refuse to give credence to those false tales so freely told us, each of the other?

We hope it may lessen your anxiety to learn we are doing our upmost to soften the lot of your civilians and war prisoners within our shores, even as we rely on your goodness of heart to do the same for ours in Germany and Austria.

Do you not feel that the vast slaughter of our opposing armies is a stain on civilization and Christianity, and that still deeper horror is aroused at the thought of those innocent victims, the countless women, children, babes, old and sick, pursued by famine, disease and death in the devastated areas, both East and West?

As we saw in South Africa and the Balkan States, the brunt of modern war falls upon non-combatants, and the conscience of the world cannot bear the sight.

Is it not our mission to preserve life? Do not humanity and commonsense alike prompt us to join hands with the women of neutral countries, and urge our rulers to stay further bloodshed? Relief, however colossal, can reach but few. Can we sit still and let the helpless die in their thousands, as die they must – *unless* we rouse ourselves in the name of Humanity to save them?

There is but one way to do this. We must all urge that peace be made with appeal to Wisdom and Reason. Since in the last resort it is these which must decide the issues, can they begin too soon, if it is to save the womanhood and childhood as well as the manhood of Europe?

Even through the clash of arms we treasure our poet's vision, and already we seem to hear

> "A hundred nations swear that there shall be
> Pity and Peace and Love among the good and free."

May Christmas hasten that day. Peace on Earth is gone, but by renewal of our faith that it still reigns at the heart of things, Christmas should strengthen both you and us and all womanhood to strive for its return.

We are yours in this sisterhood of sorrow,

Laura G. Ackroyd (Sub-Editor of *Inquirer*)
Margaret Ashton (Councillor)
A. Barclay
The Hon. Lady Barlow, etc. etc.

11

Emma Goldman's Letter to the Press on Birth Control, 1916

'Among the men and women prominent in the public life of America,' Hippolyte Havel wrote in 1910, 'there are but few whose names are mentioned as often as that of Emma Goldman.'

Anarchist, journalist, drama critic, publisher of the journal *Mother Earth* and fiery advocate of workers' rights, radical education, equality for women, free love and birth control, Emma Goldman was the most famous – and, in some quarters, the most feared – woman in the opening decades of the twentieth century. Such was the alarm at her influence that she was eventually deported from the United States as 'a subversive alien'.

The author of *Anarchism and Other Essays* (which includes the pithily titled 'The Hypocrisy of Puritanism') was born in the Jewish ghetto of Kovno in Lithuania in 1869. Aged sixteen Goldman fled a forced marriage and sailed for America, settling in Rochester, New York. Earning her living as a seamstress, she came into contact with political ideas in the garment factories and cutting rooms where she worked, and began moving in socialist and anarchist circles. In 1892, her close friend the Russian-American anarchist, Alexander Berkman, was arrested after attempting to assassinate the industrialist Henry Clay Frick. Goldman herself was jailed a year later for inciting a riot.

Aside from anarchism, Goldman also campaigned rigorously for women to have access to contraception and to enjoy the liberty of a full sexual life without the burden of unwanted pregnancies or even marriage.

'Can there be anything more outrageous,' she wrote, 'than the idea that a healthy, grown woman, full of life and passion, must deny nature's demand, must subdue her most intense craving, undermine her health and break her spirit, must stunt her vision, abstain from the depth and glory of sex experience until a "good" man comes along to take her unto himself as a wife?'

The 1873 Comstock Act, named after Anthony Comstock, a puritanical social reformer who led a crusade against literature he considered obscene or immoral, had outlawed the dispensing and publishing of information about birth control in most American states. This legislation was the pretext used to arrest Goldman in New York in February 1916, although she was actually on her way to give a lecture on atheism. Upon her release she issued a letter to the national press defending her right to speak on the subject of birth control.

Mother Earth Publishing Association
20 East 125th Street
New York

My dear Sir: -

In view of the fact that the Birth Control question is now dominant before the American public, I hope that you will not permit your prejudice against anarchism and myself as its exponent to refuse me fair play. I have lived and worked in New York City for twenty-five years. On more than one occasion I have been misrepresented in the press and anarchism has been made to appear hideous and ridiculous. I am not complaining; I am merely stating a fact which you, I am sure, know as well as I.

But now the question involved in my arrest which took place Friday, February 11th, and which is to be heard Monday, February 28th is birth control, a world wide movement sponsored and supported by the greatest men and women through Europe and America, such as Prof. August Forel, Havelock Ellis, George Bernard Shaw, H.G.Wells, Dr. Drysdale in Europe and in America by Prof. Jacobi, Dr. Robinson and many others. A movement which has originated in minds of people who were both scientific and humanitarian, and which at the present time is backed by science, sociology and economic necessity. Certainly you will not refuse me a hearing in behalf of such an issue.

I have lectured on birth control for years; many times in New York and other cities, before representative audiences. At almost every meeting plain clothes men were present taking copious notes. It was therefore no secret that I am sponsoring birth control and the necessity of imparting knowledge on this most vital question.

Friday, February 4th, I again delivered this lecture in Forward Hall, New York, when three thousand people attempted to crowd the place. As a result of this popular clamor for knowledge on birth control, another meeting was arranged for Tuesday, February 8 at the New Star Casino. Again an eager throng attended. The meeting was orderly and everything went off as peacefully and intelligently as on all the other occasions when I lecture if not interfered with by the police. Then on Friday, February 11th, just as I was about to enter the Forward Hall to deliver a lecture on Atheism, a subject which has no bearing at all upon birth control, I was arrested, taken to a filthy station house, then hustled into a patrol wagon, rushed to the Clinton Street jail, there searched in the most vulgar manner by a course looking matron in the presence of two detectives, a thing which would outrage the most hardened criminal. Then I was locked up in a cell until my bondsman released me on five hundred dollars bail.

Now all this was unnecessary in as much as I am too well known in the country to run away. Besides, one who has stood the brunt for an ideal for twenty-five years is not likely to run away. A summons would have been enough. But because I happen to be Emma Goldman and the exponent of Anarchism, the whole brutality of the New York police had to be employed in dealing with me, which only goes to prove that everything else in society advances except the Police Department. I confess I was credulous enough to believe that some change had taken place since my last arrest in New York City, which was in 1906, but I discovered my mistake.

However, this is not vital, but what is of importance and that which I hope you will place before your leaders is the fact that the methods of persecution of the part of the reactionary element in New York City in relation to any modern idea pertaining to birth control have evidently not ended with the death of Anthony Comstock. His successor wanting to ingratiate himself, is leaving nothing undone to make any intelligent discussion of that vital subject possible. Unfortunately, he and the police are evidently not aware that birth control has reached such dimensions that no amount of persecution and petty chicanery can halt its sweep.

It is hardly necessary to point out that whatever may be the law on birth control, those like myself who are disseminating knowledge along that line are not doing so because of personal gain or because we consider it lewd or obscene. We do it because we know the desperate condition among the masses of workers and even professional people, when they cannot meet the demands of numerous children. It is upon that ground that I mean to make my fight when I go into court. Unless I am very much mistaken, I am sustained in my contention by the fundamental principles in America, namely, that when a law has outgrown time and necessity, it must go and the only way to get rid of the law, is to awaken the public to the fact that it has outlived its purposes and that is precisely what I have been doing and mean to do in the future.

I am planning a campaign of publicity through a large meeting in Carnegie Hall and through every other channel that will reach the intelligent American public to the fact that while I am not particularly anxious to go to jail, I should yet be glad to do so, if thereby I can add my might to the importance of birth control and the wiping off our antiquated law upon the statute.

Hoping that you will not refuse to acquaint your readers with the facts set forth here.

Sincerely yours,
Emma Goldman

12

Bertrand Russell's Letter to the *Guardian* on Conscientious Objection, 1917

At the start of the First World War, Lord Herbert Kitchener, the Secretary of State for War, issued an appeal calling on able-bodied men to enlist out of patriotic duty. This volunteer force, known as Kitchener's Army, was intended to bolster the ranks of Britain's rather meagre professional standing army in the fight against Germany's substantially mightier military forces. A million men are thought to have signed up in the first year. Despite this, such were the casualty rates that it became clear that volunteers alone would not suffice. The Liberal government, although deeply divided over the issue, passed the Military Services Act in January 1916, introducing conscription for single men aged between eighteen and forty-one. This was swiftly extended to married men in May of the same year, and in the final year of the war the age limit was raised to fifty-one. The medically unfit, clergymen, teachers and certain classes of industrial worker were exempted. Conscientious objectors, those who objected to the war on political, moral or religious grounds, might be offered civilian or non-combatant jobs.

Some 16,000 men registered as conscientious objectors, most on religious grounds. 'Conchies', as they were contemptuously dubbed by the pro-war press, were frequently ostracised by their communities. Men of service age who weren't wearing uniform faced physical or verbal abuse in the streets, and were often publicly shamed by having white feathers, a symbol of cowardice, thrown at them. Absolutists, those conscientious objectors who refused to take any role that might aid the war, and political opponents of the war faced imprisonment and could be harshly treated by the authorities.

The philosopher and mathematician Bertrand Russell, grandson of the Liberal Prime Minister Lord John Russell, and a member of the much-mythologised Bloomsbury Group, opposed the war from its outset and wrote many letters, including the one below to the *Manchester Guardian*, in favour of conscientious objection. His anti-war campaigning eventually earned him a six-month prison sentence. Many years later, in 1961, when he was eighty-nine, Russell found himself in jail again, charged with inciting the public to commit a breach of the peace during a protest against nuclear weapons. This time round his sentence was more lenient, with the octogenarian author of *A History of Western Philosophy* spending just seven days in Brixton prison.

---

17 March 1917

To the Editor of the *Manchester Guardian*.

Sir, – In your issue of March 15 there is a discussion by "Artifex"* of the position of the conscientious objector, which, while very temperate in tone, contains two sentences which I wish to reply. "Artifex" says: –

> "I think that to be a real conscientious objector a man must be, consciously or unconsciously, an extreme individualist with little sense of the solidarity of mankind and our membership one of another."

There are no doubt many kinds of reasons which lead men to become conscientious objectors, but I am convinced that the chief reason, and the most valid, is precisely that sense of "the solidarity of mankind", of "our membership one of another," which "Artifex" denies to us. It seems to me that when he wrote "mankind" he was thinking only of the Allies. But the Germans too, are included among "mankind". The conscientious objector does not believe that violence can cure violence, or that militarism can exorcise the spirit of militarism. He persists in

---

* The pseudonym of the paper's religious columnist during the First World War, Canon Peter Green.

feeling "solidarity" with those who are called "enemies", and he believes that if this feeling were more widespread among us it would do more than armies and navies can ever do to prevent the growth of aggressive Imperialism, not only among ourselves but also among potential enemies.

"Artifex" repeats the argument that the conscientious objector accepts the protection of those who are willing to fight, and that he "will accept protection from the police and from penal laws, and pay taxes which will support not only the gaol but the scaffold." But the conscientious objector only "accepts" this "protection" because there is no way of avoiding it. He has not asked for it, and does not believe it necessary. For my part, nothing would induce me to prosecute a thief and if there are any burglars among your readers they are welcome to take note of this announcement; but I shall be very much surprised if I lose as much through them as I have lost through the operation of the law. And is it not rather ironic to speak of the protection of the law to me whom it has deprived of the means of livelihood and shut up in prison for the duration of the war, with only occasional brief intervals for fresh courts-martial? Is there really such a vast gulf between Wormwood Scrubs and Ruhleben?

Yours, &c.,
Bertrand Russell
57, Gordon Square, London, W.C.

13

Wilfred Owen's Letter to his Mother on War, 1917

Posthumously hailed as 'the Orpheus of the trenches', Wilfred Owen was one of the most outstanding poets of the First World War. He died just a week before the Armistice was signed, killed while leading his men of the 2nd Battalion, Manchester Regiment during the Battle of the Sambre near Ors in France on 4 November 1918. Prior to the war, Owen had worked as an English tutor in France and wrote Romantic poetry in the vein of Keats and Shelley. After enlisting in October 1915, his experiences of the Western Front, to which he was posted in January 1917, and his friendship with the older poet Siegfried Sassoon, were to transform his poetry. Owen met Sassoon at the Craiglockhart War Hospital, near Edinburgh, in May 1917, where both men had been sent to be treated for shell shock. Sassoon had just published *The Old Huntsman and Other Poems*, his collection of poetic 'trench life sketches', and encouraged Owen to channel his own experiences of war into verse. With poems such as 'Dulce et Decorum Est', 'Futility' and 'Anthem for Doomed Youth', Owen wrote some of the finest literature to arise from this, or indeed any, war.

Owen's mother, Susan, was deeply religious, and under her tutelage, he read passages from the Bible each day as a young man. If Owen eventually became less fervid, he never lost his Christian faith, and remained close to his mother – he wrote to her throughout his short life, providing accounts such as the one below, which described the realities of life in France during the bloody and bitter winter of 1917.

Sunday Feb. 4, 1917

My own dear Mother,

I am now indeed and in truth very far behind the line; sent down to this old Town for a Course in Transport Duties. The Battalion did not get out for a rest, and since my last letter I have had another strong dose of the advanced front line.

To begin with, I have come out quite unhurt, except for a dose of dysentery, which is now passed, and a severe cold and cough which keeps me in bed today.

I have no mind to describe all the horrors of this last Tour. But it was almost wusser than the first, because in this place my Platoon had no Dug-Outs, but had to lie in the snow under the deadly wind. By day it was impossible to stand up or even to crawl about because we were behind only a little up ridge screening us from the Bosches' periscope.

We had 5 Tommy's cookers between the Platoon, but they did not suffice to melt the ice in the water-cans. So we suffered cruelly from thirst.

The marvel is that we did not all die of cold. As a matter of fact, only one of my party actually froze to death before he got back, but I am not able to tell how many have ended in hospital. I had no real casualties from shelling, though for 10 minutes every hour whizz-bangs fell a few yards short of us. Showers of soil rained on us, but no fragments of shell could find us.

I had lost my gloves in a dug-out, but I found 1 mitten on the Field; I had my Trench Coat (without lining but with a Jerkin underneath). My feet ached until they could ache no more, and so they temporarily died. I was kept warm by the ardour of life within me. I forgot hunger in the hunger for Life. The intensity of your Love reached me and kept me living. I thought of you and Mary without break all the time. I cannot say I felt any fear. We were all half crazed by the buffetting of the High Explosives. I think the most unpleasant reflection that weighed on me was the impossibility of getting back any wounded, a total impossibility all day, and frightfully difficult by night.

We were marooned on a frozen desert. There is not a sign of life on the horizon and a thousand signs of death. Not a blade of grass, not an insect; once or twice a day the shadow of a big hawk scenting carrion.

By degrees, day by day, we worked back through the reserve and support lines to the crazy village where the Battalion takes breath. While in Support we inhabited vast Bosche dug-outs (full of all kinds of souvenirs). They are so deep that they seem warm like mines! There we began to thaw. At last I got to the village and found all your dear precious letters, and the parcel of good and precious things. The lamp is perfect, your Helmet is perfect, everything was perfect.

Then I had the heavenly-dictated order to proceed on a Transport Course. Me in Transports? Aren't you? When I departed, the gloom among the rest of the Subs. and even among Captains, was a darkness that could be felt. They can't understand my luck.

It doesn't necessarily mean a job as Transport Officer straight away, but here I am, in a delightful old town, billeted in a house, with a young Scotch Officer.

True, we can get no fuel, and the very milk freezes in the jug in a few minutes. True, I am sorely bruised by riding. True, this kind of life is expensive. But I have not been so full of content since the middle of November last.

Tell Colin how we have to ride all manner of horseflesh in the School, cantering round & round for hours, without stirrups, and folding arms and doing all kinds of circus tricks. It is very amusing – to watch. Tomorrow I shall send a P.C. of this Town, which I must not name in a letter.

Hope you had numerous Field P.C's which I dropped en route to here. The Course should last 1 month!! Alas! I have missed your last letters. It has taken 3 days to get here.

Fondest love to all, & thanks for all their letters

Your own Wilfred x

P.S. I don't at all deserve the spirited approbation which Father gives me. Though I confess I like to have his kind letters immensely. I shall read them less shame-facedly in dug-outs and trenches, than I do here in this pleasant peaceful town.

Quite 10 years ago I made a study of this town & Cathedral, in the Treasury. It is all familiar now!

Auntie Emma fairly hit it when she "perceived the awful distaste underlying" my accounts. Dear Aunt was ever a shrewd Doogie!

I suppose I can endure cold, and fatigue, and the face-to-face death, as well as another; but extra for me there is the universal pervasion of Ugliness. Hideous landscapes, vile noises, foul language, even from one's own mouth (for all are devil ridden), everything unnatural, broken, blasted; the distortion of the dead, whose unburiable bodes sit outside the dug-outs all day, all night, the most execrable sights on earth: In poetry we call them the most glorious. But to sit with them all day, all night . . . and a week later to come back and find them still sitting there in motionless groups THAT is what saps the 'soldierly spirit.'

Distaste? Distaste, Quotha?

I used to consider Tankerville Street ugly, but now . . . Well, I easily forget the unpleasant, and, look you, I even have to write it down for the sake of future reminders, reminder of how incomparable is an innocent and quiet life, at home, of work creative or humdrum, with books or without books, moneyed or moneyless, in sunshine or fog, but under an inoffensive sky, that does not shriek all night with flights of shells.

Again, I have said too much. But let me repeat that I am mighty snug here, and have a goodly prospect before me now.

I am not sorry you keep in bed from time to time, but I do hope you'll soon get some sunny walks. Are you painting?

The Letter from Lancs, was from Bobby. All the brothers are in college there. Miss de la Touche is as Bobby says "supposed to be boss" of a Belgian hospital in London . . .

Again, dearest love to all. W.E.O

14

Siegfried Sassoon's Letter to *The Times* on War, 1917

The poet and author of the novel *Memoirs of a Fox-Hunting Man*, Siegfried Sassoon spent the years before the First World War living the life of a country gentleman. Having left Cambridge without taking a degree, he indulged his love of hunting and cricket, and wrote verse that appeared in self-published pamphlets that he circulated, for the most part, among his admiring peers. Although Sir Edmund Gosse, the distinguished literary editor and author of *Father and Son*, thought these early poems showed promise, it was the war that turned Sassoon into a significant poet and writer.

He enlisted in 1915 and was posted to France, where he was given the nickname 'Mad Jack' for his near-suicidal acts of bravery and he was eventually awarded the Military Cross for valour. While convalescing in Britain after being wounded in April 1917 and after the death of his friend David Cuthbert Thomas, he was brooding on the way in which the war was being conducted and wrote the following blistering attack on the military and political establishment. After declining to return to active duty, he was sent to Craiglockhart War Hospital near Edinburgh, where he first met Wilfred Owen. Sassoon did eventually return to the front but, wounded again in July 1918, he spent the remainder of the war recuperating from his injuries.

Written on 6 July 1917 and published in *The Times* on 31 July 1917

Lt. Siegfried Sassoon,
3rd Batt. Royal Welsh Fusiliers,
July, 1917.

I am making this statement as an act of wilful defiance of military authority because I believe that the war is being deliberately prolonged by those who have the power to end it. I am a soldier, convinced that I am acting on behalf of soldiers. I believe that the war upon which I entered as a war of defence and liberation has now become a war of aggression and conquest. I believe that the purposes for which I and my fellow soldiers entered upon this war should have been so clearly stated as to have made it impossible to change them and that had this been done the objects which actuated us would now be attainable by negotiation.

I have seen and endured the sufferings of the troops, and I can no longer be a party to prolong these sufferings for ends which I believe to be evil and unjust. I am not protesting against the conduct of the war, but against the political errors and insincerities for which the fighting men are being sacrificed.

On behalf of those who are suffering now, I make this protest against the deception which is being practised upon them; also I believe that I may help to destroy the callous complacency with which the majority of those at home regard the continuance of agonies which they do not share and which they have not enough imagination to realise.

15

Mahatma Gandhi's Letter To Every Englishman in India, 1920

Mohandas Karamchand Gandhi, known as Mahatma Gandhi, always cited being thrown off a train as the pivotal moment in his political awakening. He had arrived in British-ruled South Africa in 1893 as a shy young lawyer with a London education under his belt but too meek to work in the Bombay court system. Travelling from Durban to Pretoria to take up a position with a Muslim firm there, he was in possession of a first class ticket, but a white passenger had objected to sharing a compartment with an Indian.

The indignity of this experience, and much else he encountered subsequently, would see him emerge as a formidable legal champion of the rights of discriminated Indians in Natal and the Transvaal. Initially throwing himself into the establishment of an ashram on his return to India in 1915, Gandhi duly became the chief agitator for Indian independence, and campaigned for religious, political and social reform through non-violent protest. On 13 April 1919, hundreds of Indian civilians, protesting the arrest of two prominent independence campaigners, were indiscriminately fired on by the British Army in what came to be known as the Jallianwala Bagh or Amritsar Massacre. Gandhi was galvanised by the bloodshed to issue the following appeal for change in the pages of *Young India*, a weekly English-language paper he had founded earlier in the year.

To Every Englishman in India

Dear Friend,—I wish that every Englishman will see this appeal and give thoughtful attention to it.

Let me introduce myself to you. In my humble opinion no Indian has co-operated with the British Government more than I have for an unbroken period of twenty-nine years of public life in the face of circumstances that might well have turned any other man into a rebel. I ask you to believe me when I tell you that my co-operation was not based on the fear of the punishments provided by your laws or any other selfish motives. It is free and voluntary co-operation based on the belief that the sum total of the activity of the British Government was for the benefit of India. I put my life in peril four times for the sake of the Empire – at the time of the Boer War when I was in charge of the Ambulance corps whose work was mentioned in General Buller's dispatches, at the time of the Zulu revolt in Natal when I was in charge of a similar corps, at the time of the commencement of the late War when I raised an Ambulance corps and as a result of the strenuous training had a severe attack of pleurisy and, lastly, in fulfillment of my promise to Lord Chelmsford at the War Conference in Delhi, I threw myself in such an active recruiting campaign in Kaira District involving long and trying marches that I had an attack of dysentery, which proved almost fatal. I did all this in the full belief that acts such as mine must gain my country an equal status in the Empire. So late as last December I pleaded hard for a trustful co-operation. I fully believed that Mr Lloyd George would redeem his promise to the Mussalmans and that the revelations of the official atrocities in the Punjab would secure full reparation for the Punjabis. But the treachery of Mr Lloyd George and its appreciation by you, and the condonation of the Punjab atrocities, have completely shattered my faith in the good intentions of the Government and the nation which is supporting it.

But though my faith in your good intentions is gone, I recognise your bravery and I know that what you will not yield to justice and reason, you will gladly yield to bravery.

See what this Empire means to India:

Exploitations of India's resources for the benefit of Great Britain.

An ever-increasing military expenditure and a civil service the most expensive in the world.

Extravagant working of every department in utter disregard of India's poverty.

Disarmament and consequent emasculation of a whole nation, lest an armed nation might imperil the lives of a handful of you in our midst.

Traffic in intoxicating liquors and drugs for the purpose of sustaining a top-heavy administration.

Progressively repressive legislation in order to suppress an ever-growing agitation, seeking to give expression to a nation's agony.

Degrading treatment of Indians residing in your dominions, and

You have shown total disregard of our feelings by glorifying the Punjab administration and flouting the Mussalman sentiment.

I know you would not mind if we could fight and wrest the sceptre from your hands. You know that we are powerless to do that, for you have ensured our incapacity to fight in open and honourable battle. Bravery on the battlefield is thus impossible for us. Bravery of the soul still remains open to us. I know you will respond to that also. I am engaged in evoking that bravery. Non-co-operation means nothing less than training in self-sacrifice. Why should we co-operate with you when we know that, by your administration of this great country, we are being daily enslaved in an increasing degree? This response of the people to my appeal is not due to my personality. I would like you to dismiss me, and for that matter the Ali Brothers too, from your consideration. My personality will fail to evoke any response to anti-Muslim cry if I were foolish enough to raise it, as the magic name of the Ali Brothers would fail to inspire the Mussalmans with enthusiasm if they were madly to raise an anti-Hindu cry. People flock in their thousands to listen to us, because we today represent the voice of a nation groaning under iron heels. The Ali Brothers were your friends as I was, and still am. My religion forbids me to bear any ill will towards you. I would not raise my hand against you even if I had the power. I expect to conquer you only by my suffering. The Ali Brothers will certainly draw the sword, if they could, in defence of their religion and their country. But they and I have made common cause with the people of India in their attempt to voice their feelings and to find a remedy for their distress.

You are in search of a remedy to suppress this rising ebullition of national feeling. I venture to suggest to you that the only way to suppress it is to remove the causes. You have yet the power. You can repent of the wrongs done to Indians. You can compel Mr Lloyd George to redeem his promises. I assure you he has kept many escape-doors. You can compel the Viceroy to retire in favour of a better one, you can revise your ideas about Sir Michael O'Dwyer and General Dyer. You can compel the Government to summon a conference of the recognized leaders of the people duly elected by them and representing all shades of opinion so as to devise means for granting Swaraj in accordance with the wishes of the people of India.

But this you cannot do unless you consider every Indian to be in reality your equal and brother. I ask for no patronage. I merely point out to you, as a friend, an honourable solution of a grave problem. The other solution, namely repression, is open to you. I prophesy that it will fail. It has begun already. The Government has already imprisoned two brave men of Panipat for holding and expressing their opinions freely. Another is on his trail in Lahore for having expressed similar opinions. One in the Oudh District is already imprisoned. Another awaits judgment. You should know what is going on in your midst. Our propaganda is being carried on in anticipation of repression. I invite you respectfully to choose the better way and make common cause with the people of India whose salt you are eating. To seek to thwart their aspirations is disloyalty to the country.

I am,

Your faithful friend,
M.K. GANDHI

16

Virginia Woolf's Letters to the *New Statesman* on Women Artists, 1920

Essayist, modernist, novelist, key member of the Bloomsbury Group and, with her husband Leonard, co-founder of the Hogarth Press in 1917, Virginia Woolf also wrote one of the most canonical books of feminist literature. *A Room of One's Own* appeared in 1929 and was based on two papers that she read to female undergraduates in Cambridge, having been invited to speak at the Arts Society at Newnham College and the ODTAA Society at Girton College, in October 1928. Woolf never attended university and didn't obtain a degree, but the book that resulted from these talks called for the acknowledgement of a tradition of women writers and artists, one freed from the condescension of male critics. It also looked forward to an age when women writers might be liberated from domestic confinement and financial slavery.

The roots of *A Room of One's Own*, though, could arguably be traced back to a correspondence published in the *New Statesman* nearly a decade earlier. Woolf wrote to the magazine after reading an article by the literary editor Desmond MacCarthy (writing under the *nom de plume* 'Affable Hawk'), about a new book by the then popular and prolific novelist Arnold Bennett.

Bennett, author of *Anna of the Five Towns* and *Clayhanger*, had written a non-fiction book titled *Our Women*. It included a chapter called 'Are Men Superior to Women?' that might just have well have been titled 'Men Are Superior to Women'. MacCarthy favourably quoted sections from the book in his weekly 'Books in General' column. While not going so far as to read the book itself, Woolf took it upon herself to offer a few choice criticisms of both Bennett and MacCarthy's assumptions about gender, and artistic endeavour and output.

To the editor of the NEW STATESMAN – published 9 October 1920

Sir – Like most women, I am unable to face the depression and the loss of self respect which Mr Arnold Bennett's blame and Mr Orlo Williams' praise – if it is not the other way about – would certainly cause me if I read their books in the bulk. I taste them, therefore, in sips at the hands of reviewers. But I cannot swallow the teaspoonful administered in your columns last week by Affable Hawk. The fact that women are inferior to men in intellectual power, he says, "stares him in the face." He goes on to agree with with Mr Bennett's conclusion that "no amount of education and liberty of action will sensibly alter it." How, then, does Affable Hawk account for the fact which stares me, and I should have thought any other impartial observer, in the face, that the seventeenth century produced more remarkable women than the sixteenth, the eighteenth than the seventeenth, and the nineteenth than all three put together? When I compare the Duchess of Newcastle with Jane Austen, the matchless Orinda with Emily Brontë, Mrs Haywood with George Eliot, Aphra Behn with Charlotte Brontë, Jane Grey with Jane Harrison, the advance in intellectual power seems to me not only sensible but immense; the comparison with men not in the least one that inclines me to suicide; and the effects of education and liberty scarcely to be overrated. In short, though the pessimism about the other sex is always delightful and invigorating, it seems a little sanguine of Mr Bennett and Affable Hawk to indulge in it with such certainty on the evidence before them. Thus, though women have every reason to hope the intellect of the male sex is steadily diminishing, it would be unwise, until they have more evidence than the great war and the great peace supply, to announce it as a fact. In conclusion, if Affable Hawk sincerely wishes to discover a great poetess, why does he let himself be fobbed off with a possible authoress of the *Odyssey*? Naturally I cannot claim to know Greek as Mr Bennett and Affable Hawk know it, but I have been told Sappho was a woman, and that Plato and Aristotle placed her with Homer and Archilocus among the greatest of their poets.

That Mr Bennett can name fifty of the male sex who are indisputably her superiors is therefore a welcome surprise, and if he will publish their names I will promise, as an act of that submission which is so dear to my sex, not only to buy their works but, so far as my faculties allow, to learn them by heart.

– Yours. etc.,
VIRGINIA WOOLF

Virginia Woolf's follow-up letter to the *New Statesman* following a somewhat dismissive reply by 'Affable Hawk', 16 October 1920

To the Editor of the NEW STATESMAN,

Sir – To begin with Sappho. We do not, as in the hypothetical case of Burns suggested by "Affable Hawk", judge her only by her fragments. We supplant our judgement by the opinions of those to whom her works were known in their entirety. It is true that she was born 2,500 years ago. According to "Affable Hawk" the fact that no poetess of her genius has appeared from 600 B.C. to the eighteenth century proves that during that time there was no poetess of potential genius. It follows that the absence of poetesses of moderate merit during that period proves that there were no women writers of potential mediocracy. There was no Sappho; but also until the seventeenth or eighteenth century, there was no Marie Corelli and no Mrs Barclay.

To account for the complete lack not only of good women writers but also of bad women writers I can conceive no reason unless it be that there was some external restraint upon their powers. For "Affable Hawk" admits that there have always been women of second or third rate ability. Why, unless they were forcibly prohibited, did they not express these gifts in writing, music, or painting? The case of Sappho, though so remote, throws, I think, a little light upon the problem. I quote J.A. Symonds:

> "Several circumstances contributed to aid the development of lyric poetry in Lesbos. The customs of the Aeolians

> permitted more social and domestic freedom than was common in Greece. Aeolian women were not confined to the harem like Ionians, or subjected to the rigorous discipline of the Spartans. While mixing freely with male society, they were highly educated and accustomed to express their sentiments to an extent unknown elsewhere in history – until, indeed, the present time."

And now to skip from Sappho to Ethel Smyth.

"There was nothing else [but intellectual inferiority] to prevent down the ages, so far as I can see, women who always played, sang and studied music, producing as many musicians from among their number as men have done," says "Affable Hawk". Was there nothing to prevent Ethel Smyth from going to Munich? Was there no opposition from her father? Did she find that the playing, singing and study of music which well-to-do families provided for their daughters was such as to fit them to become musicians? Yet Ethel Smyth was born in the nineteenth century. There are no great women painters, says "Affable Hawk", though painting is now within their reach. It is within their reach – if that is to say there is sufficient money after the sons have been educated to permit of paints and studios for the daughters and no family reason requiring their presence at home. Otherwise they must make a dash for it and disregard a species of torture more exquisitely painful, I believe, than any that man can imagine. And this is in the twentieth century. But "Affable Hawk" argues that a great creative mind would triumph over obstacles such as these [. . .] It seems to me indisputable that the conditions which make it possible for a Shakespeare to exist are that he shall have had predecessors in his art, shall make one of a group where art is freely discussed and practised, and shall himself have the utmost freedom of action and experience. Perhaps in Lesbos, but never since, have these conditions been the lot of women. "Affable Hawk" then names several men who have triumphed over poverty and ignorance. His first example is Isaac Newton. Newton was the son of a farmer: he was sent to grammar school; he objected to working on the farm; an uncle, a clergyman, advised that he should be exempted and prepared for college; and at the age of nineteen he was sent to Trinity College, Cambridge. Newton that is to say, had to encounter about the same amount of opposition that the daughter of a country solicitor encounters who wishes to go to Newnham in the year 1920. But his discouragement is not increased by the works of Mr Bennett, Mr Orlo Williams and "Affable Hawk."

Putting that aside, my point is that you will not get a bigger Newton until you have produced a considerable number of lesser Newtons. "Affable Hawk" will, I hope, not accuse me of cowardice if I do not take up your space with an enquiry into the careers of Laplace, Faraday, and Herschel, nor compare the lives and achievements of Aquinas and St. Theresa, nor decide whether it was Mill or his friends who was mistaken about Mrs Taylor. The fact, as I think we shall agree, is that women from the earliest times to the present day have brought forth the entire population of the universe. This occupation has taken much time and strength. It has also brought them into subjection to men, and incidentally – if that were to the point – bred in them some of the most loveable and admirable qualities of the race.

My difference with "Affable Hawk" is not that he denies the present intellectual equality of men and women. It is that he, with Mr Bennett, asserts that the mind of woman is not sensibly affected by education and liberty; that it is incapable of the highest achievements; and that it must remain forever in the condition in which it now is. I must repeat that the fact that women have improved (which "Affable Hawk" now seems to admit) shows that they may still improve; for I cannot see why a limit should be set to their improvement in the nineteenth century rather than in the one hundred and nineteenth. But it is not education only that is needed. It is that women should have liberty of experience; that they should differ from men without fear and express their differences openly (for I do not agree with "Affable Hawk" that men and women are alike): that all activity of the mind should be so encouraged that there will always be in existence a nucleus of women who think, invent, imagine, and create as freely as men do, and with little fear of ridicule and condescension. These conditions, in my view of great importance, are impeded by such statements as those of "Affable Hawk" and Mr Bennett, for a man has still much greater facilities than a woman for making his views known and respected. Certainly I cannot doubt that if such opinions prevail in the future we shall remain in a condition of half-civilised barbarism. At least that is how I define an eternity of dominion on the one hand and of servility on the other. For the degradation of being a slave is only equalled by the degradation of being a master.

Yours, etc.,
Virginia Woolf

My religion forbids me to bear any ill will towards you. I would not raise my hand against you even if I had the power. I expect to conquer you only by my suffering.

Mahatma Gandhi

17
Various Women's Letters to Marie Stopes on Birth Control, 1921

Marie Stopes was a pioneering sexologist, the founder of Britain's first birth control clinic and author of the controversial 1918 bestselling manual on marriage, *Married Love*, which was subsequently banned in America for obscenity. The following year, she produced a short pamphlet entitled *A Letter to Working Mothers*. Aimed squarely at working-class women, it explained 'the facts of life' and contraception in simple language. As many doctors and health workers refused to distribute it, Stopes issued appeals in the popular press for women – and indeed men – to write to her for advice. Deluged with letters, a collection of this correspondence was published as *Mother England* in 1929.

Stopes's membership of the Eugenics Society and her views on how women might breed healthier babies make her a complicated figure to place in the history of female emancipation. But, as the below examples of the letters she received show, the levels of ignorance about the most basic of biological functions were often heartbreaking. However problematic some of her views might have been, by raising awareness of family planning, she helped promote discussion about how women could be liberated from unwanted pregnancies and take greater control of their lives.

22 March 1921
South Wales

Mrs RGH to Marie C. Stopes

I hope you will excuse me for taking the liberty of writing you in this way as I know no other way of doing so I was reading *Lloyds News* on Sunday and I read about what you are going to do and about the Mothers Clinic that you have opened what I would like to know is how I can save having any more children as I think I have done my duty to my Country having had 13 children 9 boys and 4 girls and I have 6 boys alive now and a little girl who will be 3 year old in may I burried a dear little baby girl 3 weeks old who died from the strain of whooping cough the reason I write this is I cannot look after the little one like I would like to as I am getting very stout and cannot bend to bath them and it do jest kill me to carry them in the shawl I have always got one in my arms and another clinging to my apron and it is such a lot of work to wash and clean of us all and it is such a lot you have got to pay for someone to do a day's washing or a bit of scrubbing if I was only thin I would not grumble and as my Husband and myself is not so very old I am afraid we should have some more children . . . I was 19 when I married so you can see by the family I have had that I have not had much time for pleasure and it is telling on me now I suffer very bad with varrecoss veines in my legs and my ankles gives out and I jest drops down. I am pleased to tell you I received one of those Willow plates from the *News of the World* for Mother of the Year, so I think I have told you all my troubles . . .

Yours truly
Mrs RGH

Could I hear from you personally. I sorely need advice concerning birth control. I have only been married Four years and have just given birth for the Fifth time and it has made us desperately poor financially as my husband's wages are but small. It is through my weakness of body that I became pregnant every single time we submit to Marital Rights. I would be grateful to the end of my days if you would save me any further distress.

Your very truly

I am writing on behalf of my wife to see if you would enlighten her on Birth Control. She has had nine children of whom three are alive only her sisters keep tell her to stop having Children but they wont give her any knowledge they just say that can stop her having them i have asked there husband and they say they dont do anything my wife has two sister each has one Child only so if they have any knowledge they keep it to themselfs so i appeal to you for the sake of the Children we have and my wife to let us have the knowledge we ought to have. I am yours in unity

I would like to know if you can advice me what to do. I am a married woman with a family of small children, I was very ill over my last baby. I was under the Doctor here all the time I was pregnant with my heart, not only that I started with hemorage from the mouth, the consequence was I had not strength to bring the baby, my life was despaired of for quite a while but thank God I cam through after a struggle. Now the Doctor has advised me to have no more family but did not give me a remedy, please Dr, can you tell me what to do, I am terrible afraid, not because of children, but of my other little ones I have, they are all such Babes, if anything should happen to me over bringing another one in the world, as I have had 9 and 6 are boys, I don't think I have done so bad, and I really think it is enough for any woman to have, my husband goes to sea, he is what they call a Deck Hand on a trawler and gets £2 2 per week my rent is 11/- a week, my oldest boy is turning 14 at Christmas and has managed to bring me a few shillings working on the Docks amongst the fish, I really cant give the children all they should have to make them fine and Healthy . . . Yours Truly

18

Amelia Earhart's Letter to her Future Husband on Marriage, 1931

Reflecting on her initial encounter with her future husband, the publisher George Putnam, Amelia Earhart, the pioneering aviator and proto-feminist, maintained, 'I just didn't like him.' The pair first met in 1928 when Putnam was looking for a woman, the *first* woman, to join a flight across the Atlantic. Flushed by the success of publishing *We*, Charles Lindbergh's record of his first solo flight from New York to Paris, he believed that a woman's story of a similar voyage might also become a bestseller. Once the trip was agreed, and much to her chagrin, Putnam began brashly touting Earhart as 'Lady Lindy'.

Earhart, born in Atchison, Kansas, in 1897, was already by this time an accomplished flyer, having taken to the skies aged twenty-three in Long Beach, California. Forced into the role of backseat passenger on this historic flight from Newfoundland to Wales, she complained about being little more than 'a sack of potatoes'. Nevertheless, *20 Hours and 40 Minutes*, her account of the voyage, sold in its thousands, despite being largely concocted by Putnam and his minions.

A year later, Earhart made her own solo flight across the Atlantic and became the first woman to fly solo across the continental US and back again. Having derided marriage as 'a cage', she issued the below letter in response to a proposal from the recently divorced Putnam, who was much older than her. In it she stipulated the terms of any future marriage arrangement; he later described it as 'brutal in its frankness but beautiful in its honesty'.

Earhart and her navigator Fred Noonan disappeared somewhere over the Pacific Ocean near Howland Island during an attempt to make a circumnavigational flight of the globe in 1937.

7 February 1931

Noank
Connecticut
The Square House
Church Street

Dear GPP

There are some things which should be writ before we are married – things we have talked over before – most of them.

You must know again my reluctance to marry, my feeling that I shatter thereby chances in work which means most to me. I feel the move just now as foolish as anything I could do. I know there may be compensations but have no heart to look ahead.

On our life together I want you to understand I shall not hold you to any midaeval code of faithfulness to me nor shall I consider myself bound to you similarly. If we can be honest I think the difficulties which arise may best be avoided should you or I become interested deeply (or in passing) in anyone else.

Please let us not interfere with the other's work or play, nor let the world see our private joys or disagreements. In this connection I may have to keep some place where I can go to be myself, now and then, for I cannot guarantee to endure at all times the confinement of even an attractive cage.

I must exact a cruel promise and that is you will let me go in a year if we find no happiness together.

I will try to do my best in every way and give you that part of me you know and seem to want.

A.E.

19

Yevgeny Zamyatin's Letter to Joseph Stalin on Artistic Freedom, 1931

Trained as a naval engineer and exiled twice by the Tsarist regime for publishing subversive literature, Yevgeny Zamyatin was the author of the first novel banned in the Soviet Union. *We*, a work of dystopian science fiction that depicted life in a futuristic, technocratic authoritarian state would go on to inspire George Orwell's *1984*. But in 1921 the novel was rejected by the Soviet State Committee for Publishing – it didn't appear in Zamyatin's native Russia until 1988.

After a decade in which he often clashed with the authorities, during which time *We* had been widely translated around the world, Zamyatin appealed directly to Joseph Stalin, himself once an aspiring poet, for permission to travel outside the Soviet Union. Rather surprisingly, given the grim fates of so many other writers and artists who fell foul of the Russian censors and Stalin's aesthetic whims, his request was granted. Zamyatin lived the rest of his life in exile, dying in Paris in 1937 at the age of just fifty-three.

June, 1931

Dear Iosif Vissarionovich,

The author of the present letter, condemned to the highest penalty, appeals to you with the request for the substitution of this penalty by another. My name is probably known to you. To me as a writer, being deprived of the opportunity to write is nothing less than a death sentence. Yet the situation that has come about is such that I cannot continue my work, because no creative activity is possible in an atmosphere of systematic persecution that increases in intensity from year to year.

I have no intention of presenting myself as a picture of injured innocence. I know that among the works I wrote during the first three or four years after the revolution there were some that might provide a pretext for attacks. I know that I have a highly inconvenient habit of speaking what I consider to be the truth rather than saying what may be expedient at the moment.

Specifically, I have never concealed my attitude toward literary servility, fawning, and chameleon changes of colour: I have felt and I still feel that this is equally degrading both to the writer and to the revolution. I raised this problem in one of my articles (published in the journal *Dom Iskusstv*, No. 1, 1920) in a form that many people found to be sharp and offensive, and this served as a signal at the time for the launching of a newspaper and magazine campaign against me.

This campaign has continued, on different pretexts, to this day, and it has finally resulted in a situation that I would describe as a sort of fetishism. Just as the Christians had created the devil as a convenient personification of all evil, so the critics have transformed me into the devil of Soviet literature.

Spitting at the devil is regarded as a good deed, and everyone spat to the best of his ability. In each of my published works, these critics have inevitably discovered some diabolical intent. In order to seek it out, they have even gone to the length of investing me with prophetic gifts: thus, in one of my tales ('God'), published in the journal *Letopis* in 1916, one critic has managed to find . . . "a travesty of the revolution in connection with the transition to the NEP". In the story "The Healing of the Novice Erasmus," written in 1920, another critic (Mashbits-Verov) has discerned "a parable about leaders who had grown wise after the NEP." Regardless of the content of the given work, the very fact of my signature has become a sufficient reason for declaring the work criminal.

Last March the Leningrad Oblit took steps to eliminate any remaining doubts of this. I had edited Sheridan's comedy *The School for Scandal* and written an article about his life and work for the Academy Publishing House. Needless to say, there was nothing of a scandalous nature that I said or could have said in this article. Nevertheless, the Oblit not only banned the article, but even forbade the publisher to mention my name as editor of the translation. It was only after I complained to Moscow, and after the Glavlit had evidently suggested that such naively open actions are, after all, inadmissible, that permission was granted to publish the article and even my criminal name.

I have cited this fact because it shows the attitude toward me in a completely exposed, so to speak, chemically pure form. Of a long array of similar facts, I shall mention only one more, involving, not a chance article, but a full-length play that I have worked on for almost three years. I felt confident that this play – the tragedy *Attila* – would finally silence those who were intent on turning me into some sort of an obscure artist. I seemed to have every reason for such confidence. My play had been read at a meeting of the Artistic Council of the Leningrad Bolshoi Dramatic Theatre. Among those present at this meeting were representatives of eighteen Leningrad factories. Here are excerpts from their comments (taken from the minutes of the meeting of May 1, 1928). The representative of the Volodarsky Plant said: "This is a play by a contemporary author, treating the subject of the class struggle in ancient times, analogous to that of our own era . . . Ideologically, the play is quite acceptable . . . It creates a strong impression and eliminates the reproach that contemporary playwrights do not produce good plays" . . . The representative of the Lenin Factory noted the revolutionary character of the play and said that "in its artistic level, the play reminds us of Shakespeare's works . . . It is tragic, full of action, and will capture the viewer's attention." The representative of the Hydro-Mechanical Plant found "every moment in the play strong and absorbing," and recommended its opening on the theatre's anniversary.

Let us say that the comrade workers overdid it in regard to Shakespeare. Nevertheless, Maxim Gorky has written that he considers the play "highly valuable both in a literary and social sense," and that "its heroic tone and heroic plot are most useful for our time." The play was accepted for production by the theatre; it was passed by the Glavrepertkom; and after that . . .

Was it shown to the audience of workers who had rated it so highly? No. After that the play, already half-rehearsed by the theatre, already announced in posters, was banned at the insistence of the Leningrad Oblit. The death of my tragedy *Attila* was a genuine tragedy to me. It made entirely clear to me the futility of any attempt to alter my situation, especially in view of the well-known affair involving my novel *We* and Pilnyak's *Mahogany*, which followed soon after. Of course, any falsification is permissible in fighting the devil. And so, the novel, written nine years earlier, in 1920, was set side by side with *Mahogany* and treated as my latest, newest work.

The manhunt organized at the time was unprecedented in Soviet literature and even drew notice in the foreign press. Everything possible was done to close to me all avenues for further work. I became an object of fear to my former friends, publishing houses and theatres. My books were banned from the libraries. My play (*The Flea*), presented with invariable success by the Second Studio of the Moscow Art Theatre for four seasons, was withdrawn from the repertory. The publication of my collected works by the Federation Publishing House was halted. Every publishing house which attempted to issue my works was immediately placed under fire; this happened to Federatsiia ['Federation'], Zemlia i Fabrika ['Land and Factory'], and particularly to the Publishing House of Leningrad Writers. This latter took the risk of retaining me on its editorial board for another year and ventured to make use of my literary experience by entrusting me with the stylistic editing of works by young writers including Communists. Last spring the Leningrad branch of the RAPP succeeded in forcing me out of the board and putting an end to this work. The *Literary Gazette* triumphantly announced this accomplishment, adding quite unequivocally: " . . . the publishing house must be preserved, but not for the Zamyatins."

The last door to the reader was closed to Zamyatin. The writer's death sentence was pronounced and published. In the Soviet Criminal Code the penalty second to death is deportation of the criminal from the country. If I am in truth a criminal deserving punishment, I nevertheless do not think that I merit so grave a penalty as literary death. I therefore ask that this sentence be changed to deportation from the USSR and that my wife be allowed to accompany me.

But if I am not a criminal, I beg to be permitted to go abroad with my wife temporarily, for at least one year, with the right to return as soon as it becomes possible in our country to serve great ideas in literature without cringing before little men, as soon as there is at least a partial change in the prevailing view concerning the role of the literary artist. And I am confident that this time is near, for the creation of the material base will inevitably be followed by the need to build the superstructure, an art and a literature truly worthy of the revolution.

I know that life abroad will be extremely difficult for me, as I cannot become a part of the reactionary camp there; this is sufficiently attested by my past membership in the Russian Social Democratic [Bolshevik] Party in Tsarist days, imprisonment, two deportations, trial in wartime for an anti-militarist novella.

I know that while I have been proclaimed a Right winger here because of my habit of writing according to my conscience rather than according to command, I shall sooner or later probably be declared a Bolshevik for the same reason abroad.

But even under the most difficult conditions there, I shall not be condemned to silence; I shall be able to write and to publish, even, if need be, in a language other than Russian. If circumstances should make it impossible (temporarily, I hope) for me to be a Russian writer, perhaps I shall be able, like the Pole Joseph Conrad, to become for a time an English writer, especially since I have already written about England in Russian (the satirical story "The Islanders" and others), and since it is not much more difficult for me to write in English than it is in Russian.

Ilya Ehrenburg, while remaining a Soviet writer, has long been working chiefly for European literature for translation into foreign languages. Why, then, should I not be permitted to do what Ehrenburg has been permitted to do? And here I may mention yet another name that of Boris Pilnyak. He has shared the role of devil with me in full measure; he has been the major target of the critics; yet he has been allowed to go abroad to take a rest from this persecution. Why should I not be granted what has been granted to Pilnyak?

I might have tried to motivate my request for permission to go abroad by other reasons as well more usual, though equally valid. To free myself of an old chronic illness (colitis), I have to go abroad for a cure; my personal presence is needed abroad to help stage two of my plays, translated into English and Italian (*The Flea* and *The Society of Honorary Bell Ringers*, already produced in Soviet theatres); moreover, the planned production of these plays will make it possible for me not to burden the People's Commissariat of Finances with the request for foreign exchange.

All these motives exist. But I do not wish to conceal that the basic reason for my request for permission to go abroad with my wife is my hopeless position here as a writer, the death sentence that has been pronounced upon me as a writer here at home. The extraordinary consideration which you have given other writers who appealed to you leads me to hope that my request will also be granted.

20

Albert Einstein's Correspondence with Sigmund Freud on Global Peace, 1932

Albert Einstein, the theoretical physicist who developed the general theory of relativity, and Sigmund Freud, the founding father of psychoanalysis, seem only to have met briefly, in 1927. But in 1931, with the encouragement of the League of Nations' International Institute of Intellectual Cooperation, a body formed to bolster public debate between prominent intellectuals of the day, the pair exchanged a series of letters, in which they considered how war might be ended and global peace established.

Why War?

Caputh near Potsdam, 30th July, 1932

Dear Mr Freud,

The proposal of the League of Nations and its International Institute of Intellectual Co-operation at Paris that I should invite a person, to be chosen by myself, to a frank exchange of views on any problem that I might select affords me a very welcome opportunity of conferring with you upon a question which, as things now are, seems the most insistent of all the problems civilization has to face. This is the problem: Is there any way of delivering mankind from the menace of war? It is common knowledge that, with the advance of modern science, this issue has come to mean a matter of life and death for Civilization as we know it; nevertheless, for all the zeal displayed, every attempt at its solution has ended in a lamentable breakdown.

I believe, moreover, that those whose duty it is to tackle the problem professionally and practically are growing only too aware of their impotence to deal with it, and have now a very lively desire to learn the views of men who, absorbed in the pursuit of science, can see world problems in the perspective distance lends. As for me, the normal objective of my thought affords no insight into the dark places of human will and feeling. Thus, in the enquiry now proposed, I can do little more than to seek to clarify the question at issue and, clearing the ground of the more obvious solutions, enable you to bring the light of your far-reaching knowledge of man's instinctive life to bear upon the problem. There are certain psychological obstacles whose existence a layman in the mental sciences may dimly surmise, but whose interrelations and vagaries he is incompetent to fathom; you, I am convinced, will be able to suggest educative methods, lying more or less outside the scope of politics, which will eliminate these obstacles.

As one immune from nationalist bias, I personally see a simple way of dealing with the superficial (i.e., administrative) aspect of the problem: the setting up, by international consent, of a legislative and judicial body to settle every conflict arising between nations. Each nation would undertake to abide by the orders issued by this legislative body, to invoke its decision in every dispute, to accept its judgements unreservedly and to carry out every measure the tribunal deems necessary for the execution of its decrees. But here, at the outset, I come up against a difficulty; a tribunal is a human institution which, in proportion as the power at its disposal is inadequate to enforce its verdicts, is all the more prone to suffer these to be deflected by extrajudicial pressure. This is a fact with which we have to reckon; law and might inevitably go hand in hand, and juridical decisions approach more nearly the ideal justice demanded by the community (in whose name and interests these verdicts are pronounced) in so far as the community has effective power to compel respect of its juridical ideal. But at present we are far from possessing any supranational organization competent to render verdicts of incontestable authority and enforce absolute submission to the execution of its verdicts. Thus I am led to my first axiom: The quest of international security involves the unconditional surrender by every nation, in a certain measure, of its liberty of action – its sovereignty that is to say – and it is clear beyond all doubt that no other road can lead to such security.

The ill success, despite their obvious sincerity, of all the efforts made during the last decade to reach this goal leaves us no room to doubt that strong psychological factors are at work, which paralyse these efforts. Some of these factors are not far to seek. The craving for power which characterizes the governing class in every nation is hostile to any limitation of the national sovereignty. This political power-hunger is often supported by the activities of another group, whose aspirations are on purely mercenary, economic lines. I have especially in mind that small but determined group, active in every nation, composed of individuals who, indifferent to social considerations and restraints, regard warfare, the manufacture and sale of arms, simply as an occasion to advance their personal interests and enlarge their personal authority.

But recognition of this obvious fact is merely the first step towards an appreciation of the actual state of affairs. Another question follows hard upon it: How is it possible for this small clique to bend the will of the majority, who stand to lose and suffer by a state of war, to the service of their ambitions? (In speaking of the majority, I do not exclude soldiers of every rank who have chosen war as their profession, in the belief that they are serving to defend the highest interests of their race, and that attack is often the best method of defence.) An obvious answer to this question would seem to be that the minority, the ruling class at present, has the schools and press, usually the Church as well, under its thumb. This enables it to organize and sway the emotions of the masses, and make its tool of them.

Yet even this answer does not provide a complete solution. Another question arises from it: How is it these devices succeed so well in rousing men to such wild enthusiasm, even to sacrifice their lives? Only one answer is possible. Because man has within him a lust for hatred and destruction. In normal times this passion exists in a latent state, it emerges only in unusual circumstances; but it is a comparatively easy task to call it into play and raise it to the power of a collective psychosis. Here lies, perhaps, the crux of all the complex factors we are considering, an enigma that only the expert in the lore of human instincts can resolve.

And so we come to our last question. Is it possible to control man's mental evolution so as to make him proof against the psychoses of hate and destructiveness? Here I am thinking by no means only of the so-called uncultured masses. Experience proves that it is rather the so-called 'Intelligentsia' that is most apt to yield to these disastrous collective suggestions, since the intellectual has no direct contact with life in the raw, but encounters it in its easiest synthetic form – upon the printed page.

To conclude: I have so far been speaking only of wars between nations; what are known as international conflicts. But I am well aware that the aggressive instinct operates under other forms and in other circumstances. (I am thinking of civil wars, for instance, due in earlier days to religious zeal, but nowadays to social factors; or, again, the persecution of racial minorities.) But my insistence on what is the most typical, most cruel and extravagant form of conflict between man and man was deliberate, for here we have the best occasion of discovering ways and means to render all armed conflicts impossible.

I know that in your writings we may find answers, explicit or implied, to all the issues of this urgent and absorbing problem. But it would be of the greatest service to us all were you to present the problem of world peace in the light of your most recent discoveries, for such a presentation well might blaze the trail for new and fruitful modes of action.

Yours very sincerely,
A. Einstein

Vienna, September, 1932.

Dear Mr Einstein,

When I heard that you intended to invite me to an exchange of views on some subject that interested you and that seemed to deserve the interest of others besides yourself, I readily agreed. I expected you to choose a problem on the frontiers of what is knowable today, a problem to which each of us, a physicist and a psychologist, might have our own particular angle of approach and where we might come together from different directions upon the same ground. You have taken me by surprise, however, by posing the question of what can be done to protect mankind from the curse of war. I was scared at first by the thought of my – I had almost written 'our' – incapacity for dealing with what seemed to be a practical problem, a concern for statesmen. But I then realized that you had raised the question not as a natural scientist and physicist but as a philanthropist: you were following the promptings of the League of Nations just as Fridtjof Nansen, the polar explorer, took on the work of bringing help to the starving and homeless victims of the World War. I reflected, moreover, that I was not being asked to make practical proposals but only to set out the problem of avoiding war as it appears to a psychological observer. Here again you yourself have said almost all there is to say on the subject. But, though you have taken the wind out of my sails, I shall be glad to follow in your wake and content myself with confirming all you have said by amplifying it to the best of my knowledge – or conjecture.

You begin with the relation between Right and Might. There can be no doubt that that is the correct starting-point for our investigation. But may I replace the word 'might' by the balder and harsher word 'violence'? Today right and violence appear to us as antitheses. It can easily be shown, however, that the one has developed out of the other; and, if we go back to the earliest beginnings and see how that first came about, the problem is easily solved. You must forgive me if in what follows I go over familiar and commonly accepted ground as though it were new, but the thread of my argument requires it.

It is a general principle, then, that conflicts of interest between men are settled by the use of violence. This is true of the whole animal kingdom, from which men have no business to exclude themselves. In the case of men, no doubt, conflicts of opinion occur as well which may reach the highest pitch of abstraction and which seem to demand some other technique for their settlement. That, however, is a later complication. To begin with, in a small human horde, it was superior muscular strength which decided who owned things or whose will should prevail. Muscular strength was soon supplemented and replaced by the use of tools: the winner was the one who had the better weapons or who used them the more skilfully. From the moment at which weapons were introduced, intellectual superiority already began to replace brute muscular strength; but the final purpose of the fight remained the same – one side or the other was to be compelled to abandon his claim or his objection by the damage inflicted on him and by the crippling of his strength. That purpose was most completely achieved if the victor's violence eliminated his opponent permanently – that is to say, killed him. This had two advantages: he could not renew his opposition and his fate deterred others from following his example. In addition to this, killing an enemy satisfied an instinctual inclination which I shall have to mention later. The intention to kill might be countered by a reflection that the enemy could be employed in performing useful services if he were left alive in an intimidated condition. In that case the victor's violence was content with subjugating him instead of killing him. This was a first beginning of the idea of sparing an enemy's life, but thereafter the victor had to reckon with his defeated opponent's lurking thirst for revenge and sacrificed some of his own security.

Such, then, was the original state of things: domination by whoever had the greater might – domination by brute violence or by violence supported by intellect. As we know, this regime was altered in the course of evolution. There was a path that led from violence to right or law. What was that path? It is my belief that there was only one: the path which led by way of the fact that the superior strength of a single individual could be rivalled by the union of several weak ones. '*L'union fait la force.*' Violence could be broken by union, and the power of those who were united now represented law in contrast to the violence of the single individual. Thus we see that right is the might of a community. It is still violence, ready to be directed against any individual who resists it; it works by the same methods and follows the same purposes. The only real difference lies in the fact that what prevails is no longer the violence of an individual but that of a community. But in order that the transition from violence to this new right or justice may be effected, one psychological condition must be fulfilled. The union of the majority must be a stable and lasting one. If it were only brought about for the purpose of combating a single dominant individual and were dissolved after his defeat, nothing would have been accomplished. The next person who thought himself superior in strength would once more seek to set up a dominion by violence and the game would be repeated ad infinitum. The community must be maintained permanently, must be organized, must draw up regulations to anticipate the risk of rebellion and must institute authorities to see that those regulations – the laws – are respected and to superintend the execution of legal acts of violence. The recognition of a community of interests such as these leads to the growth of emotional ties between the members of a united group of people – communal feelings which are the true source of its strength.

Here, I believe, we already have all the essentials: violence overcome by the transference of power to a larger unity, which is held together by emotional ties between its members. What remains to be said is no more than an expansion and a repetition of this.

The situation is simple so long as the community consists only of a number of equally strong individuals. The laws of such an association will determine the extent to which, if the security of communal life is to be guaranteed, each individual must surrender his personal liberty to turn his strength to violent uses. But a state of rest of that kind is only theoretically conceivable. In actuality the position is complicated by the fact that from its very beginning the community comprises elements of unequal strength – men and women, parents and children – and soon, as a result of war and conquest, it also comes to include victors and vanquished, who turn into masters and slaves. The justice of the community then becomes an expression of the unequal degrees of power obtaining within it; the laws are made by and for the ruling members and find little room for the rights of those in subjection. From that time forward there are two factors at work in the community which are sources of unrest over matters of law but tend at the same time to a further growth of law. First, attempts are made by certain of the rulers to set themselves above the prohibitions which apply to everyone – they seek, that is, to go back from a dominion of law to a dominion of violence. Secondly, the oppressed members of the group make constant efforts to obtain more power and to have any changes that are brought about in that direction recognized in the laws – they press forward, that is, from unequal justice to equal justice for all. This second tendency becomes especially important if a real shift of power occurs within a community, as may happen as a result of a number of historical factors. In that case right may gradually adapt itself to the new distribution of power; or, as is more frequent, the ruling class is unwilling to recognize the change, and rebellion and civil war follow, with a temporary suspension of law and new attempts at a solution by violence, ending in the establishment of a fresh rule of law. There is yet another source from which modifications of law may arise, and one of which the expression is invariably peaceful: it lies in the cultural transformation of the members of the community. This, however, belongs properly in another connection and must be considered later.

Thus we see that the violent solution of conflicts of interest is not avoided even inside a community. But the everyday necessities and common concerns that are inevitable where people live together in one place tend to bring such struggles to a swift conclusion and under such conditions there is an increasing probability that a peaceful solution will be found. Yet a glance at the history of the human race reveals an endless series of conflicts between one community and another or several others, between larger and smaller units – between cities, provinces, races, nations, empires – which have almost always been settled by force of arms. Wars of this kind end either in the spoliation or in the complete overthrow and conquest of one of the parties. It is impossible to make any sweeping judgement upon wars of conquest. Some, such as those waged by the Mongols and Turks, have brought nothing but evil. Others, on the contrary, have contributed to the transformation of violence into law by establishing larger units within which the use of violence was made impossible and in which a fresh system of law led to the solution of conflicts. In this way the conquests of the Romans gave the countries round the Mediterranean the priceless *pax Romana*, and the greed of the French kings to extend their dominions created a peacefully united and flourishing France. Paradoxical as it may sound, it must be admitted that war might be a far from inappropriate means of establishing the eagerly desired reign of 'everlasting' peace, since it is in a position to create the large units within which a powerful central government makes further wars impossible. Nevertheless it fails in this purpose, for the results of conquest are as a rule short-lived: the newly created units fall apart once again, usually owing to a lack of cohesion between the portions that have been united by violence. Hitherto, moreover, the unifications created by conquest, though of considerable extent, have only been partial, and the conflicts between these have called out more than ever for violent solution. Thus the result of all these warlike efforts has only been that the human race has exchanged numerous, and indeed unending, minor wars for wars on a grand scale that are rare but all the more destructive.

If we turn to our own times, we arrive at the same conclusion which you have reached by a shorter path. Wars will only be prevented with certainty if mankind unites in setting up a central authority to which the right of giving judgement upon all conflicts of interest shall be handed over. There are clearly two separate requirements involved in this: the creation of a supreme agency and its endowment with the necessary power. One without the other would be useless. The League of Nations is designed as an agency of this kind, but the second condition has not been fulfilled: the League of Nations has no power of its own and can only acquire it if the members of the new union, the separate States, are ready to resign it. And at the moment there seems very little prospect of this. The institution of the League of Nations would, however, be wholly unintelligible if one ignored the fact that here was a bold attempt such as has seldom (perhaps, indeed, never on such a scale) been made before. It is an attempt to base upon an appeal to certain idealistic attitudes of mind the authority (that is, the coercive influence) which otherwise rests on the possession of power. We have seen that a community is held together by two things: the compelling force of violence and the emotional ties (identifications is the technical name) between its members. If one of the factors is absent, the community may possibly be held together by the other.

The ideas that are appealed to can, of course, only have any significance if they give expression to important affinities between the members, and the question arises of how much strength such ideas can exert. History teaches us that they have been to some extent effective. For instance, the Panhellenic idea, the sense of being superior to the surrounding barbarians – an idea which was so powerfully expressed in the Amphictyonic Council, the Oracles and the Games – was sufficiently strong to mitigate the customs of war among Greeks, though evidently not sufficiently strong to prevent warlike disputes between the different sections of the Greek nation or even to restrain a city or confederation of cities from allying itself with the Persian foe in order to gain an advantage over a rival. The community of feeling among Christians, powerful though it was, was equally unable at the time of the Renaissance to deter Christian States, whether large or small, from seeking the Sultan's aid in their wars with one another. Nor does any idea exist today which could be expected to exert a unifying authority of the sort. Indeed it is all too clear that the national ideals by which nations are at present swayed operate in a contrary direction. Some people are inclined to prophesy that it will not be possible to make an end of war until Communist ways of thinking have found universal acceptance. But that aim is in any case a very remote one today, and perhaps it could only be reached after the most fearful civil wars. Thus the attempt to replace actual force by the force of ideas seems at present to be doomed to failure. We shall be making a false calculation if we disregard the fact that law was originally brute violence and that even today it cannot do without the support of violence.

I can now proceed to add a gloss to another of your remarks. You express astonishment at the fact that it is so easy to make men enthusiastic about a war and add your suspicions that there is something at work in them – an instinct for hatred and destruction – which goes halfway to meet the efforts of the warmongers. Once again, I can only express my entire agreement. We believe in the existence of an instinct of that kind and have in fact been occupied during the last few years in studying its manifestations. Will you allow me to take this opportunity of putting before you a portion of the theory of the instincts which, after much tentative groping and many fluctuations of opinion, has been reached by workers in the field of psychoanalysis?

According to our hypothesis human instincts are of only two kinds: those which seek to preserve and unite – which we call 'erotic', exactly in the sense in which Plato uses the word 'Eros' in his *Symposium*, or 'sexual', with a deliberate extension of the popular conception of 'sexuality' – and those which seek to destroy and kill and which we group together as the aggressive or destructive instinct. As you see, this is in fact no more than a theoretical clarification of the universally familiar opposition between Love and Hate which may perhaps have some fundamental relation to the polarity of attraction and repulsion that plays a part in your own field of knowledge. But we must not be too hasty in introducing ethical judgements of good and evil. Neither of these instincts is any less essential than the other; the phenomena of life arise from the concurrent or mutually opposing action of both. Now it seems as though an instinct of the one sort can scarcely ever operate in isolation; it is always accompanied – or, as we say, alloyed – with a certain quota from the other side, which modifies its aim or is, in some cases, what enables it to achieve that aim. Thus, for instance, the instinct of self-preservation is certainly of an erotic kind, but it must nevertheless have aggressiveness at its disposal if it is to fulfil its purpose. So, too, the instinct of love, when it is directed towards an object, stands in need of some contribution from the instinct for mastery if it is in any way to obtain possession of that object. The difficulty of isolating the two classes of instinct in their actual manifestations is indeed what has so long prevented us from recognizing them.

If you will follow me a little further, you will see that human actions are subject to another complication of a different kind. It is very rarely that an action is the work of a single instinctual impulse (which must in itself be compounded of Eros and destructiveness). In order to make an action possible there must be as a rule a combination of such compounded motives. This was perceived long ago by a specialist in your own subject, a Professor G.C. Lichtenberg who taught physics at Göttingen during our classical age – though perhaps he was even more remarkable as a psychologist than as a physicist. He invented a Compass of Motives, for he wrote: 'The motives that lead us to do anything might be arranged like the thirty-two winds and might be given names in a similar way: for instance, "bread-bread-fame" or "fame-fame-bread".' So that when human beings are incited to war they may have a whole number of motives for assenting – some noble and some base, some which are openly declared and others which are never mentioned. There is no need to enumerate them all. A lust for aggression and destruction is certainly among them: the countless cruelties in history and in our everyday lives vouch for its existence and its strength. The satisfaction of these destructive impulses is of course facilitated by their admixture with others of an erotic and idealistic kind. When we read of the atrocities of the past, it sometimes seems as though the idealistic motives served only as an excuse for the destructive appetites; and sometimes – in the case, for instance, of the cruelties of the Inquisition – it seems as though the idealistic motives had pushed themselves forward in consciousness, while the destructive ones lent them an unconscious reinforcement. Both may be true.

I fear I may be abusing your interest, which is after all concerned with the prevention of war and not with our theories. Nevertheless I should like to linger for a moment over our destructive instinct, whose popularity is by no means equal to its importance. As a result of a little speculation, we have come to suppose that this instinct is at work in every living creature and is striving to bring it to ruin and to reduce life to its original condition of inanimate matter. Thus it quite seriously deserves to be called a death instinct, while the erotic instincts represent the effort to live. The death instinct turns into the destructive instinct when, with the help of special organs, it is directed outwards, on to objects. The organism preserves its own life, so to say, by destroying an extraneous one. Some portion of the death instinct, however, remains operative within the organism, and we have sought to trace quite a number of normal and pathological phenomena to this internalization of the destructive instinct. We have even been guilty of the heresy of attributing the origin of conscience to this diversion inwards of aggressiveness. You will notice that it is by no means a trivial matter if this process is carried too far: it is positively unhealthy. On the other hand if these forces are turned to destruction in the external world, the organism will be relieved and the effect must be beneficial. This would serve as a biological justification for all the ugly and dangerous impulses against which we are struggling. It must be admitted that they stand nearer to Nature than does our resistance to them for which an explanation also needs to be found. It may perhaps seem to you as though our theories are a kind of mythology and, in the present case, not even an agreeable one. But does not every science come in the end to a kind of mythology like this? Cannot the same be said to-day of your own Physics?

For our immediate purpose then, this much follows from what has been said: there is no use in trying to get rid of men's aggressive inclinations. We are told that in certain happy regions of the earth, where nature provides in abundance everything that man requires, there are races whose life is passed in tranquillity and who know neither coercion nor aggression. I can scarcely believe it and I should be glad to hear more of these fortunate beings. The Russian Communists, too, hope to be able to cause human aggressiveness to disappear by guaranteeing the satisfaction of all material needs and by establishing equality in other respects among all the members of the community. That, in my opinion, is an illusion. They themselves are armed to-day with the most scrupulous care and not the least important of the methods by which they keep their supporters together is hatred of everyone beyond their frontiers. In any case, as you yourself have remarked, there is no question of getting rid entirely of human aggressive impulses; it is enough to try to divert them to such an extent that they need not find expression in war.

Our mythological theory of instincts makes it easy for us to find a formula for indirect methods of combating war. If willingness to engage in war is an effect of the destructive instinct, the most obvious plan will be to bring Eros, its antagonist, into play against it. Anything that encourages the growth of emotional ties between men must operate against war. These ties may be of two kinds. In the first place they may be relations resembling those towards a loved object, though without having a sexual aim. There is no need for psycho-analysis to be ashamed to speak of love in this connection, for religion itself uses the same words: 'Thou shalt love thy neighbour as thyself.' This, however, is more easily said than done. The second kind of emotional tie is by means of identification. Whatever leads men to share important interests produces this community of feeling, these identifications. And the structure of human society is to a large extent based on them.

A complaint which you make about the abuse of authority brings me to another suggestion for the indirect combating of the propensity to war. One instance of the innate and ineradicable inequality of men is their tendency to fall into the two classes of leaders and followers. The latter constitute the vast majority; they stand in need of an authority which will make decisions for them and to which they for the most part offer an unqualified submission. This suggests that more care should be taken than hitherto to educate an upper stratum of men with independent minds, not open to intimidation and eager in the pursuit of truth, whose business it would be to give direction to the dependent masses. It goes without saying that the encroachments made by the executive power of the State and the prohibition laid by the Church upon freedom of thought are far from propitious for the production of a class of this kind. The ideal condition of things would of course be a community of men who had subordinated their instinctual life to the dictatorship of reason. Nothing else could unite men so completely and so tenaciously, even if there were no emotional ties between them. But in all probability that is a Utopian expectation. No doubt the other indirect methods of preventing war are more practicable, though they promise no rapid success. An unpleasant picture comes to one's mind of mills that grind so slowly that people may starve before they get their flour.

The result, as you see, is not very fruitful when an unworldly theoretician is called in to advise on an urgent practical problem. It is a better plan to devote oneself in every particular case to meeting the danger with whatever means lie to hand. I should like, however, to discuss one more question, which you do not mention in your letter but which specially interests me. Why do you and I and so many other people rebel so violently against war? Why do we not

For the degradation of being a slave is only equalled by the degradation of being a master.

Virgina Woolf

accept it as another of the many painful calamities of life? After all, it seems to be quite a natural thing, to have a good biological basis and in practice to be scarcely avoidable. There is no need to be shocked at my raising this question. For the purpose of an investigation such as this, one may perhaps be allowed to wear a mask of assumed detachment. The answer to my question will be that we react to war in this way because everyone has a right to his own life, because war puts an end to human lives that are full of hope, because it brings individual men into humiliating situations, because it compels them against their will to murder other men, and because it destroys precious material objects which have been produced by the labours of humanity. Other reasons besides might be given, such as that in its present-day form war is no longer an opportunity for achieving the old ideals of heroism and that owing to the perfection of instruments of destruction a future war might involve the extermination of one or perhaps both of the antagonists. All this is true, and so incontestably true that one can only feel astonished that the waging of war has not yet been unanimously repudiated. No doubt debate is possible upon one or two of these points. It may be questioned whether a community ought not to have a right to dispose of individual lives; every war is not open to condemnation to an equal degree; so long as there exist countries and nations that are prepared for the ruthless destruction of others, those others must be armed for war. But I will not linger over any of these issues; they are not what you want to discuss with me, and I have something different in mind. It is my opinion that the main reason why we rebel against war is that we cannot help doing so. We are pacifists because we are obliged to be for organic reasons. And we then find no difficulty in producing arguments to justify our attitude.

No doubt this requires some explanation. My belief is this. For incalculable ages mankind has been passing through a process of evolution of culture. (Some people, I know, prefer to use the term 'civilization'.) We owe to that process the best of what we have become, as well as a good part of what we suffer from. Though its causes and beginnings are obscure and its outcome uncertain, some of its characteristics are easy to perceive. It may perhaps be leading to the extinction of the human race, for in more than one way it impairs the sexual function; uncultivated races and backward strata of the population are already multiplying more rapidly than highly cultivated ones. The process is perhaps comparable to the domestication of certain species of animals and it is undoubtedly accompanied by physical alterations; but we are still unfamiliar with the notion that the evolution of civilization is an organic process of this kind. The psychical modifications that go along with the process of civilization are striking and unambiguous. They consist in a progressive displacement of instinctual aims and a restriction of instinctual impulses. Sensations which were pleasurable to our ancestors have become indifferent or even intolerable to ourselves; there are organic grounds for the changes in our ethical and aesthetic ideals. Of the psychological characteristics of civilization two appear to be the most important: a strengthening of the intellect, which is beginning to govern instinctual life, and an internalization of the aggressive impulses, with all its consequent advantages and perils. Now war is in the crassest opposition to the psychical attitude imposed on us by the process of civilization, and for that reason we are bound to rebel against it; we simply cannot any longer put up with it. This is not merely an intellectual and emotional repudiation; we pacifists have a constitutional intolerance of war, an idiosyncrasy magnified, as it were, to the highest degree. It seems, indeed, as though the lowering of aesthetic standards in war plays a scarcely smaller part in our rebellion than do its cruelties.

And how long shall we have to wait before the rest of mankind become pacifists too? There is no telling. But it may not be Utopian to hope that these two factors, the cultural attitude and the justified dread of the consequences of a future war, may result within a measurable time in putting an end to the waging of war. By what paths or by what side-tracks this will come about we cannot guess. But one thing we can say: whatever fosters the growth of civilization works at the same time against war.

I trust you will forgive me if what I have said has disappointed you, and I remain, with kindest regards,

Sincerely yours,
Sigmund Freud

21

The Mayor of Jarrow J.W. Thompson's Letter Calling for Support for Unemployed Men, 1936

With the closure of its steelworks and shipyard in the early 1930s, Jarrow, on the south bank of the River Tyne, was an industrial town left with little industry. Its unemployment rate rocketed to 80 per cent and the local MP, Ellen Wilkinson, nicknamed 'Red Ellen' for her radical views, helped to organise a march by 200 men of the nearly 300 miles to London, to draw attention to their plight and present a petition demanding jobs to parliament. On the eve of their departure the Mayor, J.W. Thompson, drafted a letter to go out to trade union organisations and other councils, calling on them to offer aid.

While often warmly supported by those they met on their twenty-six-day trek south, on finally reaching Westminster the marchers were rebuffed by the Conservative Prime Minister Stanley Baldwin, who claimed to be too busy to see them.

5th October, 1936

Borough of Jarrow
Mayor's Parlour,
Town Hall,
Jarrow,
Co., Durham.
To the Secretary

Dear Sir,

UNEMPLOYMENT IN JARROW

Jarrow, a Tyneside borough of 35,000 inhabitants, is fighting to extricate itself from industrial depression. Without parallel, for fifteen years the town has suffered from persistent unemployment which had impoverished homes and brought widespread distress. The Town Council has pledged itself to make the biggest non-political fight for work ever waged in history by a single town. The sympathy – more than that – the assistance of the whole country is needed in this fight, and as Mayor in this difficult period I appeal to your Society/Party for support.

Prior to 1921, the town's workers were employed at the Palmer Shipbuilding & Iron Works, which gave employment to over 8,000 people. These works are in process of demolition, and in place of the hum of industry all that is heard are the reports of shattering explosions of blasting materials in connexion with the breaking up of the works. In these works, where formerly thousands of persons were employed, only 100 or so are employed on a makeshift scheme.

In recent years, thirteen industries have been forced to close down. The famous shipyard was bought by National Shipbuilders Security Limited, a company formed by certain shipbuilders, the objects of which included the buying up of shipyards the owners of which were willing to sell, and the subsequent disposal of the yards subject to a restriction against shipbuilding therein for a period of 40 years. The Palmer Yard was so disposed of by the company. The Council objected to H.M. Government against the imposition of such a restriction which, it was urged, was contrary to public policy, but unfortunately the Government did not intervene, and the yard remains closed. Thus was destroyed the tradition created by the honest work of thousands of shipbuilders.

About eighteen months ago, the town was heartened by the appearance of a scheme for the re-establishment of the steel works. From statements made, it appeared that the scheme had the support of H.M. Government and the Town Council lent to it all the support in its power. In a debate on the 30th June, 1936, in the House of Commons it became clear that there was obstruction to the scheme by the British Iron & Steel Federation, a body composed of representatives of proprietors of steelworks, and as a result of sending a deputation to the President of the Board of Trade, it clearly appeared that the scheme would not proceed.

An appeal was made to the Government to remove the obstacle placed in the way of progress by the Federation, but no response was forthcoming.

To meet the grave situation which was so brought about, the Council – Conservatives, Socialists, and Liberals – is taking all available steps. The absence of any prospect of resuscitation of industry otherwise, impels the Council to call upon the Government to realise its responsibilities to the town. Toward this end there is in course of preparation a town's petition to the House of Commons praying that the Government actively assist the resuscitation of industry in the town. The Council is prepared, itself, if the Government will give it power and assistance, to be the organiser of the resuscitation of industry.

Unanimously the Council decided to lead a protest march to London to convey their petition for work, firmly convinced that Government intervention can remove the obstacles which are preventing willing industrialists from establishing works which, without throwing men in other parts of the country out of work, could absorb practically all Jarrow's unemployed.

There are now 5,000 persons out of work in the town. Every year 300 boys leave school with practically no chance of a job, and no future before them. There are now over 400 youths between the ages of 16 and 18 years of age who have never done a day's work in their lives.

The results of this continued unemployment are seen not only in the breaking up of family life, and the semi-starvation of the people, but in the rate which has risen as the rateable value of the town has decreased, and also in the closing down of shops. Jarrow was once a prosperous shopping centre. Now there are rows of closed shops. The loss of industries has reduced the rateable value by £21,000.

An even more tragic tale is told by the vital statistics, issued by our Health Department, which is the hardest worked in the country, and in which we have spent large sums of money in a struggle to check disease which follows upon the heels of unemployment.

Although Jarrow is a well situated town near the sea we have one of the largest infantile mortality rates in the country, namely 95.82 per thousand births against an average for similar towns of 53, and over the five years from 1930 to 1934 the average death rate from tuberculosis is 1.04 per thousand, and from pneumonia 1.38. Work for the town will check the evils of unemployment which these figures indicate. Fine and independent men with a fine industrial record behind them are waiting for their share in the revival of national prosperity which so far has passed them by.

We are out to gain no political capital, only work for our people. I appeal to your Society/Party to support us. We need all the financial assistance for the march we can get, and I shall be glad to receive any donations it may care to send.

I hope that by the response to the appeals which are being sent out all over the country, including through the press, to local authorities, trade unions and other organisations, it will be shown that Jarrow is not a forgotten town.

Yours faithfully,
J.W. Thompson
Mayor of Jarrow

22

Antonio Gramsci's Letters to his Wife and Son from Prison on Family, 1936

In 1928, Antonio Gramsci, the Sardinian-born journalist, political theorist, agitator and former leader of the Italian Communist Party, was sentenced to twenty years imprisonment by Benito Mussolini's fascist judiciary, for undermining the Italian state. Although poorly treated in prison, he was at least permitted to write, and produced thirty-three volumes and 3,000 pages of his thoughts on history, philosophy and economics. Stowed away by a cellmate and published posthumously as the *Prison Notebooks*, Gramsci's ideas, and especially his concept of hegemony, in which a powerful group, government or regime's dominance seeps into the surrounding culture as a whole, would go on to influence a diverse range of political thinkers.

Alongside these writings, Gramsci also penned some 500 letters; among the most touching are those to his Russian wife, Iulca, and their two sons, Delio and Giuliano. The latter child was born after his father's internment and he would never meet him. After losing all his teeth during his first two years in prison, Gramsci's health went from bad to worse: eventually unable to digest solid food, he suffered a massive cerebral haemorrhage in 1937 and died, aged only 46.

Clinica Quisisana Rome,
November 24, 1936

Dear Iulca,

I have decided to write you a letter like a professor, filling it with pedantry from top to bottom just to make you laugh.

Usually, I'm pedantic when I don't mean to be. Because of the many times that I've been subject to censorship during the events of these past ten years, I've had to develop a style to suit the circumstances. Let me tell you a little story that will make you laugh and also illustrate my state of mind. One time, when Delio was little, you wrote a charming letter to show me how he was beginning to learn about geography and to have a sense of direction. You described him lying in bed in a north-south position, repeating that in the direction of his head lived races who used dog carts, to the left was China and to the right Austria, the legs pointed to the Crimea, and so on. In order to have this letter in my possession, I had to defend it without having even read it to see what the whole issue was about! The director of the prison kept me for an hour, wanting to know what secret messages were contained in it! "What is Kitai, and what's this about Austria?" "Who are these men who make dogs drag their cars?" I had quite a time trying to offer a plausible explanation for for all this, without having even glanced at the letter. Finally, I asked the man brusquely, "But aren't you married? Surely, you understand how a mother might write to her distant husband about their child". He gave me the letter on the spot. (He was married but had no children.) The episode is a silly but significant one. Since I knew that the director would go on reading my letters afterward with the same acrimonious, suspicious pedantry he had shown in my case, I was forced to develop a prison style of writing, which I may never be able to shake off after so many years of disciplining what I wish to say. I could tell you about similar episodes and other things, but would do it only to make you laugh. It might be very saddening to have the many trials of the past years laid out before you. Your letter cheered me up, instead. I can't remember when you last wrote so gaily . . . and with so few mistakes.

Sweetheart, think a bit and then write me a long letter about the Malyshi,* without being too objective. By the way, your sententious aphorism. "To write a report (?!) about the children's

---

* *Malyshi* is Russian for the 'little ones'.

life would be to destroy the essence of it" is one of the most ridiculous things I've ever heard! . . . I don't want a report – I am not a policeman – but only your subjective impressions. Dearest, I'm so isolated that your letters are like bread, they nourish me: pedantry could never do that. Why do you continue to measure out the rations that you send me? When all is said and done, it looks as though you are far more pedantic and professorial than I, only you prefer not to admit it. A miserable fellow like me writes asking for a description of his children's life and you answer from your safe hide-out, "Oh no, to write about the children's life would be to destroy the essence of it." Isn't this pedantry? It's pedantry of the worst kind. Think a bit, and then you'll see that I'm right.

Sweet Iulca, I send you a tender hug.

Antonio

Clinic Quisisana Rome

Darling Delio,

I am feeling a little tired and can't write you a long letter. Go on writing to me about everything that interests you in school. I think you like history, as I liked it at your age, because it concerns living men; and everything that concerns them – as many men as possible, all the men in the world, insofar as they unite society and work and strive to improve themselves – must necessarily interest you more than anything else. But is this the case for you? A hug.

Antonio

23

Anaïs Nin's Letter to Robert Duncan on Homosexuality, 1939

The French-born novelist and diarist Anaïs Nin once maintained that 'the only abnormality is the incapacity to love'. A sexually liberated woman in a less socially forgiving age, Nin had a long-standing affair with Henry Miller, the author of *Tropic of Cancer* and a dedicated bohemian spirit. At a Christmas party in Woodstock, Upstate New York, according to one source 'thrown by some impresarios of the maverick art scene', Nin first met the poet Robert Duncan. Nin recorded in her diary that Duncan was 'a strikingly beautiful boy [with] a faunish expression and a slight deviation in one eye, which made him seem to be looking always beyond and around you'.

At the time of their meeting, his homosexuality seems to have been causing him much distress. Nin wrote to him, urging him to accept and to take pride in who and what he was. This was not such an easy thing at a time when homosexuality was considered a criminal offence by the US military and was illegal in many parts of the world. Duncan, though, heeded Nin's advice. His taboo-breaking essay, 'The Homosexual in Society', was published in 1944 and he began living openly as a gay man.

December 1939

To Robert,

You refuse to free yourself from serving in the Army by declaring your homosexuality. And by this you will live a double lie, for you are also against war. At the same time you feel burdened with guilt. Our only prison is that of guilt. Guilt is the negative aspect of religion. We lost our religion but we kept the guilt. We all have guilt. Even Henry has it, who seems the freest of all. Only domestic animals have guilt. We train them so. Animals in the jungle do not have it.

Everything negative should die. Jealousy as the negative form of love, fear the negative form of life.

You speak of suffering, of withdrawal, retreat. Face this suffering, for all the real suffering can save us from unreality. Real pain is human and deepening. Without real pain you will remain the child forever. The legend of Ondine tells of how she acquired a human soul the day she wept over a human love. You were caught in a web of unreality. You chose suffering in order to be awakened from your dreams, as I did. You are no longer the sleeping prince of neurosis. Don't run away from it now. If you run away from it without conquering it (I say accept the homosexuality, live it out proudly, declare it), then you will remain asleep and enchanted in a lifeless neurosis.

Anaïs

24

A.A. Milne's Letter to a Correspondent on Pacifism, 1939

The carnage and devastation of the First World War provoked a widespread revulsion against rearmament, war and militarism in general. The establishment of the League of Nations in 1920, which aimed to promote greater co-operation between nations, was greeted with enthusiasm, and the decision to admit Germany in 1926 was seen as a decisive step on the road to securing a long-term European peace. 'Never Again' was a much-repeated phrase of the inter-war years, with talk of international relations and disarmament a constant, alongside the establishment of new organisations devoted to the promotion of peace. One of the most popular, the Peace Pledge Union, was formed in 1934, following an appeal by the Reverend Dick Sheppard of St Martin-in-the-Fields, whose services were regularly broadcast on BBC Radio.

In the same year, A.A. Milne, creator of the much-loved Winnie-the-Pooh stories for children, published *Peace with Honour*, his own contribution to the cause. Like most men of his generation, Milne was a veteran of the First World War himself. He had hoped for a permanent end to war but, faced with Hitler, Milne abandoned his pacifism and argued that Nazism had to be defeated by whatever means necessary. He laid out the reasons for changing of his mind in a letter to one correspondent in December 1939.

Cotchford Farm,
Hartfield
Sussex
i. xii. 39

Dear Sir,

I am afraid that I am not with you; for I believe that war is a lesser evil than Hitlerism. I believe that Hitlerism must be killed before war can be killed. I think that it is more important to abolish war than to avoid or stop one war. I am a practical pacifist. In 1933 when I began *Peace with Honour* my only (infinitesimal) hope of ending war was to publish my views and hope that they would have time to spread before war broke out. They did not. One must try again. But since Hitler's victory will not abolish war; and since Peace now (which is the recognition of Hitlerism) will not abolish war; one must hope to be alive to try again after England's victory – and in the meantime to do all that one can to bring that about.

Yours faithfully,
A.A. Milne

25

Albert Camus' Letters to a German Friend on the Occupation, 1943–4

Albert Camus, the French-Algerian journalist, playwright, novelist, philosopher and essayist, received the Nobel Prize for Literature in 1957; tragically, he would be killed in a car accident less than three years later. At the time of his death, he had been compiling *Resistance, Rebellion, and Death*, a book of articles that included pieces written during the Second World War. While under German occupation, Camus had helped produce *Combat*, the main clandestine newspaper of the French Resistance movement, and had also written for other resistance journals. Among the pieces he resurrected from this time was a series of letters supposedly addressed to a German friend, some of which had appeared in *La Revue Libre* and *Cahiers de Libération* in 1943 and 1944.

In a preface to accompany the letters, Camus outlined the conditions in which they had been written:

> I cannot let these pages be reprinted without saying what they are. They were written and published clandestinely during the Occupation. They had a purpose, which was to throw some light on the blind battle we were then waging and thereby to make our battle more effective. They are topical writings and hence they may appear unjust . . . When the author of these letters says 'you', he means not 'you Germans' but 'you Nazis'. When he says 'we', this signifies not always 'we Frenchmen' but sometimes 'we free Europeans'. I am contrasting two attitudes, not two nations, even if, at a certain moment in history, these two nations personified two enemy attitudes. To repeat a remark that is not mine, I love my country too much to be a

nationalist . . . I loathe none but executioners. Any reader who reads the *Letters to a German Friend* in this perspective – in other words, as a document emerging from the struggle against violence – will see how I can say I don't disown a single word I have written here.

From the first letter, July 1943

You said to me: "The greatness of my country is beyond price. Anything is good that contributes to its greatness. And in a world where everything has lost its meaning, those who, like us young Germans, are lucky enough to find meaning in the destiny of our nation must sacrifice everything else." I loved you then, but at that point we diverged. "No", I told you, "I cannot believe that everything must be subordinated to a single end. There are means that cannot be excused. And I should like to be able to love my country and still love justice. I don't want just any greatness for it, particularly a greatness born of blood and falsehood. I want to keep it alive by keeping justice alive." You retorted: "Well, you just don't love your country." [. . .]

We had much to overcome, first of all, the constant temptation to emulate you. For there is always something in us that yields to instinct, to contempt for intelligence, to the cult of efficiency. Our great virtues eventually become tiresome to us. We become ashamed of our intelligence, and sometimes we imagine some barbarous state where truth would be effortless. But the cure for this is easy; you are there to show us what such imagining would lead to, and we mend our ways. [. . .]

Contrary to what we used to think, the spirit is of no avail against the sword, but the spirit together with the sword will always win over the sword alone. That is why we have now accepted the sword, after making sure that the spirit was on our side. We had first to see people die and to run the risk of dying ourselves. [. . .] One really possesses only what one has paid for. We have paid dearly, and we have not finished paying. But we have our certainties, our justifications, our justice; your defeat is inevitable. [. . .]

We are fighting for fine distinctions, but the kind of distinctions that are as important as the man himself. We are fighting for the distinction between sacrifice and mysticism, between energy and violence, between strength and cruelty, for that even finer distinction between the true and the false, between the man of the future and the cowardly gods you revere.

From the second letter, December 1943

This is what separated us from you; we made demands. You were satisfied to serve the power of your nation and we dreamed of giving ours her truth. It was enough for you to serve the politics of reality whereas, in our wildest aberrations, we still had a vague conception of the politics of honour, which we recognize today. When I say "we" I am not speaking of our rulers. But a ruler hardly matters. [. . .]

What is truth, you used to ask? To be sure, but at least we know what falsehood is; that is just what you have taught us. What is spirit? We know its contrary, which is murder. What is man? There I stop you, for we know. Man is that force which ultimately cancels all tyrants and gods. He is the force of evidence. Human evidence is what we must preserve [. . .] If nothing had any meaning, you would be right. But there is something that still has meaning. [. . .]

"I am ashamed for that man, and I am pleased to think that no French priest would have been willing to make his God abet murder." That was true. The chaplain simply felt as you do. It seemed natural to him to make even his faith serve his country. Even the gods are mobilized in your country. They are on your side, as you say, but only as a result of coercion. You no longer distinguish anything; you are but a single impulse. And now you are fighting with the resources of blind anger, with your mind on weapons and feats of arms rather than on ideas, stubbornly confusing every issue and following your obsession. We, on the other hand, started from the intelligence and its hesitations. We were powerless against wrath. But now our detour is finished. It took only a dead child for us to add wrath to intelligence, and now we are two against one.

From the third letter, April 1944

That idea of Europe that you took from the best among us and distorted has consequently become hard for us to keep alive in all its original force. [. . .] You speak of Europe but the difference is that for you Europe is a property, whereas we feel that we belong to it. [. . .] You say "Europe", but you think in terms of potential soldiers, granaries, industries brought to heel, intelligence under control. Am I going too far? But at least I know that when you say "Europe", even in your best moments, when you let yourselves be carried away by your own lies, you cannot keep yourselves from thinking of a cohort of docile nations led by a lordly Germany toward a fabulous and bloody future. I should like you to be fully aware of the difference. For you Europe is an expanse encircled by seas and mountains, dotted with dams, gutted with mines, covered with harvests, where Germany is playing a game in which her fate alone is at stake. But for us Europe is a home of the spirit where for the last twenty centuries the most amazing adventure of the human spirit has been going on. It is the privileged arena in which Western man's struggle against the world, against the gods, against himself is today reaching its climax. As you see, there is no common denominator. [. . .] Your Europe is not the right one. There is nothing there to unite or inspire. Ours is a joint adventure that we shall continue to pursue, despite you, with the inspiration of intelligence.

Sometimes on a street corner, in the brief intervals of the long struggle that involves us all, I happen to think of all those places in Europe I know well. It is a magnificent land mouded by suffering and history. I relive those pilgrimages I once made with all the men of the West: the roses in the cloisters of Florence, the gilded bulbous domes of Krakow, the Hradschin and its dead palaces, the contorted statues of the Charles Bridge over the Vltava, the delicate gardens of Salzburg. All those flowers and stones, those hills and those landscapes where men's time and the world's time have mingled old trees and monuments! My memories have fused together such superimposed images to make a single face, which is the face of my true native land. [. . .] It never occurred to me that someday we should have to liberate them from you. And even now, at certain moments of rage and despair, I am occasionally sorry that the roses continue to grow in the cloister of San Marco and the pigeons drop clusters from the Cathedral of Salzburg, and the red geraniums grow tirelessly in the little cemeteries of Silesia.

But at other moments, and they are the only ones that count, I delight in this. For all those landscapes, those flowers and those ploughed fields, the oldest of lands, show every spring that there are things you cannot choke in blood. [. . .] So I know that everything in Europe, both landscape and spirit, calmly negates you without feeling any rash hatred, but with the calm strength of victory. The weapons the European spirit can use against you are the same as reside in this soil constantly reawakening in blossoms and harvests. The battle we are waging is sure victory because it is as obstinate as spring.

And, finally, I know that all will not be over when you are crushed. Europe will still have to be established. It always has to be established.

From the fourth letter, July 1944

For a long time we both thought that this world had no ultimate meaning and that consequently we were cheated. I still think so in a way. But I came to different conclusions from the ones you used to talk about, which, for so many years now, you have been trying to introduce into history. I tell myself now that if I had really followed your reasoning, I ought to approve what you are doing. And this is so serious that I must stop and consider it, during this summer night so full of promises for us and threats for you.

You never believed in the meaning of this world, and you therefore deduced the idea that everything was equivalent and that good and evil could be defined according to one's wishes. You supposed that in the absence of any human or divine code the only values were those of the animal world – in other words, violence and cunning. Hence you concluded that man was negligible and that his soul could be killed, that in the maddest of histories the only pursuit for the individual was the adventure of power and his own morality, the realism of conquests. And, to tell the truth, I, believing I thought as you did, saw no valid argument to answer you except a fierce love of justice which, after all, seemed to me as unreasonable as the most sudden passion.

Where lay the difference? Simply that you readily accepted despair and I never yielded to it. Simply that you saw the injustice of our condition to the point of being willing to add to it, whereas it seemed to me that man must exalt justice in order to fight against eternal injustice, create happiness in order to protest against the universe of unhappiness. [. . .]

I continue to believe that this world has no ultimate meaning. But I know that something in it has a meaning and that is man, because he is the only creature to insist on having one. This world has at least the truth of man, and our task is to provide its justification against fate itself. And it has no justification but man; hence he must be saved if we want to save the idea we have of life. [. . .]

Our difficult achievement consisted in following you into war without forgetting happiness. And despite the clamours and the violence, we tried to preserve in our hearts the memory of a happy sea, of a remembered hill, the smile of a beloved face. For that matter, this was our best weapon, the one we shall never put away. For as soon as we lost it we should be as dead as you are. But we now know that the weapons of happiness cannot be forged without considerable time and too much blood. [. . .]

You are the man of injustice and, and there is nothing in the world that my heart loathes so much. But now I know the reasons for what was once only passion. I am fighting you because your logic is as criminal as your heart. And in the horror you have lavished upon us for four years, your reason plays as large a part as your instinct. This is why my condemnation will be sweeping; you are already dead as far as I am concerned. But at the very moment when I am judging your horrible behaviour, I shall remember that you and we started from the same solitude, that you and we, with all Europe, are caught in the same tragedy of intelligence. And, despite yourselves, I shall still apply to you the name of man. [. . .] I can tell you that at the very moment when we are going to destroy you without pity, we still feel no hatred for you. [. . .]

Our strength lies in thinking as you do about the essence of the world, in rejecting no aspect of the drama that is ours. But at the same time we have saved the idea of man at the end of this disaster of the intelligence, and that idea gives us the undying courage to believe in rebirth. To be sure, the accusation we make against the world is not mitigated by this. We paid so dear for this new knowledge that our condition continues to seem desperate to us. Hundreds of thousands of men assassinated at dawn, the terrible walls of prisons, the soil of Europe reeking with millions of corpses of its sons – it took all that to pay for the acquisition of two or three slight distinctions which may have no other value than to help some among us to die more nobly. Yes, that is heart-breaking. [. . .] The dawn about to break will mark your final defeat. I know that heaven, which was indifferent to your horrible victories, will be equally indifferent to your defeat. Even now I expect nothing from heaven. But we shall at least have helped save man from the solitude to which you wanted to relegate him. Because you scorned such faith in mankind, you are the men who, by thousands, are going to die solitary. Now, I can say farewell to you.

26

Zora Neale Hurston's Letter to Countee Cullen on Segregation, 1943

By the time of her death in the ward of a Florida welfare home in 1960, Zora Neale Hurston was penniless and all but forgotten. But, thanks to the championing of writers such as Alice Walker, this anthropologist, novelist and leading figure of the Harlem Renaissance, who had been buried in an unmarked grave in a segregated cemetery, has since come to be acknowledged as one of the foremost chroniclers of the twentieth-century African-American experience. Her novel *Their Eyes Were Watching God* is now considered a classic and is widely studied. However, it was only in 2018 that *Barracoon*, a non-fiction portrait of Oluale Kossola, the final survivor of the last known slave ship from Africa, and one of her most-cherished projects, was finally published. Composed from her interviews with him, the book was completed in 1931 and rejected by every publisher she showed it to – she would later write about it in an article entitled 'What White Publishers Won't Print'.

In this letter to her fellow Harlem Renaissance writer, the poet Countee Cullen, who had briefly been married to Yolande Du Bois, the daughter of W.E.B. Du Bois, Hurston discusses her feelings about white liberals, lynching and segregation.

March 5, 1943

Dear Countee:

Thanks a million for your kind letter. I am always proud to have a word of praise from you because your friendship means a great deal to me. It means so much to me because I have never known you to make an insincere move, neither for personal gain, nor for malice growing out of jealousy of anyone else. Then too, you are my favorite poet now as always since you began to write. I have always shared your approach to art. That is, you have written from within rather than to catch the eye of those who were making the loudest noise for the moment. I know that hitch-hiking on band-wagons has become the rage among Negro artists for the last ten years at least, but I have never thumbed a ride and can feel no admiration for those who travel that way. I have pointed you out on numerous occasions as one whose integrity I respected, and whose example I wished to follow.

Now, as to segregation, I have no viewpoint on the subject particularly, other than a fierce desire for human justice. The rest of it is up to the individual. Personally, I have no desire for white association except where I am sought and the pleasure is mutual. That feeling grows out of my own self-respect. However blue the eye or yellow the hair, I see no glory to myself in the contact unless there is something more than the accident of race. Any other viewpoint would be giving too much value to a mere white hide. I have offended several "liberals" among the whites by saying this bluntly. I have been infuriated by having them ask me outright, or by strong implication if I am not happy over the white left wing associating with Negroes. I always say no. Then I invariably ask why the association should give a Negro so much pleasure? Why any more pleasure than with a black "liberal"? They never fail to flare up at that which proves that they are paying for the devout worship that many Negroes give them in the cheap coin of patronage, which proves that they feel the same superiority of race that they claim to deny. Otherwise, why assume that they have done a noble deed by having contact with Negroes? Countee, I have actually had some of them to get real confidential and point out that I can be provided with a white husband by seeing things right! White wives and husbands have been provided for others, etc.

I invariably point out that getting hold of white men has always been easy. I don't need any help to do that. I only wish that I could get everything else so easily as I can get white men. I am utterly indifferent to the joy of other Negroes who feel that a marriage across the line is compensation for all things, even conscience. The South must laugh and gloat at the spectacle and say "I told you so! That is a black person's highest dream." If a white man or woman marries a Negro for love that is all right with me, but a Negro who considers himself or herself paid off and honored by it is a bit too much for me to take. So I shall probably never become a "liberal." Neither shall I ever let myself be persuaded to have my mind made up for me by a political job. I mean to live and die by my own mind. If that is cowardly, then I am a coward. When you come to analyze it, Countee, some of the stuff that has passed as courage among Negro "leaders" is nauseating. Oh, yes, they are right there with the stock phrases, which the white people are used to and expect, and pay no attention to anymore. They are rather disappointed if you do not use them. But if you suggest something real just watch them back off from it. I know that the Anglo-Saxon mentality is one of violence. Violence is his religion. He has gained everything he has by it, and respects nothing else. When I suggest to our "leaders" that the white man is not going to surrender for mere words what he has fought and died for, and that if we want anything substantial we must speak with the same weapons, immediately they object that I am not practical.

No, no indeed. The time is not ripe, etc. etc. Just point out that we are suffering injustices and denied our rights, as if the white people did not know that already! Why don't I put something about lynchings in my books? As if all the world did not know about Negroes being lynched! My stand is this: either we must do something about it that the white man will understand and respect, or shut up. No whiner ever got any respect or relief. If some of us must die for human justice, then let us die. For my own part, this poor body of mine is not so precious that I would not be willing to give it up for a good cause. But my own self-respect refuses to let me go to the mourner's bench. Our position is like a man sitting on a tack and crying that it hurts, when all he needs to do is to get up off it. A hundred Negroes killed in the streets of Washington right now could wipe out Jim Crow in the nation so far as the law is concerned, and abate it at least 60% in actuality. If any of our leaders start something like that then I will be in it body and soul. But I shall never join the cry-babies.

You are right in assuming that I am indifferent to the pattern of things. I am. I have never liked stale phrases and bodyless courage. I have the nerve to walk my own way, however hard, in my search for reality, rather than climb upon the rattling wagon of wishful illusions.

I suppose you have seen my denial of the statements of Douglas Gilbert of the *World-Telegram*. I know I made him sore. He is one of the type of "liberals" I spoke of. They are all Russian and want our help to put them in power in the U.S. but I know that we would be liquidated soon after they were in. They will have to get there the best way they can for all I care.

Cheerio, good luck, and a happy encounter (with me) in the near future.

Sincerely,
Zora

If some of us must die for human justice, then let us die. For my own part, this poor body of mine is not so precious that I would not be willing to give it up for a good cause.

Zora Neale Hurston

27

George Orwell's Letter to Noel Willmett on Totalitarianism, 1944

In the spring of 1944, after eight years of childless marriage, George Orwell and Eileen Blair were making plans to adopt a son. *Animal Farm*, Orwell's recently completed satirical fable, had finally found a publisher, after being rejected by at least four houses. The author of *Down and Out in Paris and London* and *Homage to Catalonia* was also by then the literary editor of *Tribune*, the left-leaning paper, for which he composed a weekly column entitled 'As I Please'. Professionally busy and on the brink of a major literary success and impending parenthood, Orwell's mind, perhaps naturally, turned to the state of the world to come.

A letter written to one of his critics at this time revealed that, some three years before he finally sat down to write it, the building blocks of his great dystopian novel, *1984*, were already in his mind.

A month after this letter was posted, the Orwells' flat in Mortimer Crescent, Kilburn, was hit by a German V-1 rocket. No one was injured, but the building suffered substantial damage and the couple were forced to seek new accommodation in Canonbury Square, Islington. Further tragedies were to come – Eileen died during a routine operation in 1945 and, by the time *1984* was published in June 1949, Orwell had contracted tuberculosis and had less than a year to live.

To Noel Willmett

18 May 1944
10a Mortimer Crescent NW 6

Dear Mr Willmett,

Many thanks for your letter. You ask whether totalitarianism, leader-worship etc. are really on the up-grade and instance the fact that they are not apparently growing in this country and the USA.

I must say I believe, or fear, that taking the world as a whole these things are on the increase. Hitler, no doubt, will soon disappear, but only at the expense of strengthening (a) Stalin, (b) the Anglo-American millionaires and (c) all sorts of petty führers of the type of de Gaulle. All the national movements everywhere, even those that originate in resistance to German domination, seem to take non-democratic forms, to group themselves round some superhuman führer (Hitler, Stalin, Salazar, Franco, Gandhi, De Valera are all varying examples) and to adopt the theory that the end justifies the means. Everywhere the world movement seems to be in the direction of centralised economies which can be made to 'work' in an economic sense but which are not democratically organised and which tend to establish a caste system. With this go the horrors of emotional nationalism and a tendency to disbelieve in the existence of objective truth because all the facts have to fit in with the words and prophecies of some infallible führer. Already history has in a sense ceased to exist, i.e. there is no such thing as a history of our own times which could be universally accepted, and the exact sciences are endangered as soon as military necessity ceases to keep people up to the mark. Hitler can say that the Jews started the war, and if he survives that will become official history. He can't say that two and two are five, because for the purposes of, say, ballistics they have to make four. But if the sort of world that I am afraid of arrives, a world of two or three great superstates which are unable to conquer one another, two and two could become five if the führer wished it. That, so far as I can see, is the direction in which we are actually moving, though, of course, the process is reversible.

As to the comparative immunity of Britain and the USA. Whatever the pacifists etc. may say, we have *not* gone totalitarian yet and this is a very hopeful symptom. I believe very deeply, as I explained in my book *The Lion and the Unicorn*, in the English *people* and in their capacity to centralise their economy without destroying freedom in doing so. But one must remember that Britain and the USA haven't been really tried, they haven't known defeat or severe suffering, and there are some bad symptoms to balance the good ones. To begin with there is the general indifference to the decay of democracy. Do you realise, for instance, that no one in England under 26 now has a vote and that so far as one can see the great mass of people of that age don't give a damn for this? Secondly there is the fact that the intellectuals are more totalitarian in outlook than the common people. On the whole the English intelligentsia have opposed Hitler, but only at the price of accepting Stalin. Most of them are perfectly ready for dictatorial methods, secret police, systematic falsification of history etc. so long as they feel that it is on 'our' side. Indeed the statement that we haven't a Fascist movement in England largely means that the young, at this moment, look for their führer elsewhere. One can't be sure that that won't change, nor can one be sure that the common people won't think ten years hence as the intellectuals do now. I *hope* they won't, I even trust they won't, but if so it will be at the cost of a struggle. If one simply proclaims that all is for the best and doesn't point to the sinister symptoms, one is merely helping to bring totalitarianism nearer.

You also ask, if I think the world tendency is towards Fascism, why do I support the war. It is a choice of evils – I fancy nearly every war is that. I know enough of British imperialism not to like it, but I would support it against Nazism or Japanese imperialism, as the lesser evil. Similarly I would support the USSR against Germany because I think the USSR cannot altogether escape its past and retains enough of the original ideas of the Revolution to make it a more hopeful phenomenon than Nazi Germany. I think, and have thought ever since the war began, in 1936 or thereabouts, that our cause is the better, but we have to keep on making it the better, which involves constant criticism.

Yours sincerely,
George Orwell

28

Niels Bohr's Open Letter to the United Nations on Nuclear Arms, 1950

Awarded the Nobel Prize in Physics in 1922 for his work on the hydrogen atom, the Danish scientist Niels Bohr is regarded as one the foremost physicists of the twentieth century and the pioneer of quantum theory. While some of Bohr's ideas ultimately paved the way for the creation of the atomic bomb, he had initially believed that such a use remained a distant prospect.

Although non-practising himself, Bohr's mother was Jewish and he was forced to flee Copenhagen in 1943, when the occupying Nazis began arresting Jews. He reluctantly made his way to Britain and then America, learning in due course about the rapid advances the Manhattan Project had made towards the development of a viable nuclear bomb. This alarmed Bohr. In 1944, he met both the British Prime Minister Winston Churchill and the US President Franklin D. Roosevelt, and tried to convince them that the international control of these weapons was essential for world peace. Privately deploring America's use of nuclear weapons on the Japanese cities of Hiroshima and Nagasaki in 1945, Bohr campaigned for their control following the end of the war, until his death in 1962. In 1950, he issued this thorough and thoughtful open letter to the United Nations.

Open Letter to the United Nations

Copenhagen

I address myself to the organization, founded for the purpose to further co-operation between nations on all problems of common concern, with some considerations regarding the adjustment of international relations required by modern development of science and technology. At the same time as this development holds out such great promises for the improvement of human welfare it has, in placing formidable means of destruction in the hands of man, presented our whole civilization with a most serious challenge.

My association with the American-British atomic energy project during the war gave me the opportunity of submitting to the governments concerned views regarding the hopes and the dangers which the accomplishment of the project might imply as to the mutual relations between nations. While possibilities still existed of immediate results of the negotiations within the United Nations on an arrangement of the use of atomic energy guaranteeing common security, I have been reluctant in taking part in the public debate on this question. In the present critical situation, however, I have felt that an account of my views and experiences may perhaps contribute to renewed discussion about these matters so deeply influencing international relationship.

In presenting here views which on an early stage impressed themselves on a scientist who had the opportunity to follow developments on close hand, I am acting entirely on my own responsibility and without consultation with the government of any country. The aim of the present account and considerations is to point to the unique opportunities for furthering understanding and co-operation between nations which have been created by the revolution of human resources brought about by the advance of science, and to stress that despite previous disappointments these opportunities still remain and that all hopes and all efforts must be centered on their realization.

For the modern rapid development of science and in particular for the adventurous exploration of the properties and structure of the atom, international co-operation of an unprecedented extension and intensity has been of decisive importance. The fruitfulness of the exchange of experiences and ideas between scientists from all parts of the world was a great source of encouragement to every participant and strengthened the hope that an ever closer contact between nations would enable them to work together on the progress of civilization in all its aspects.

Yet, no one confronted with the divergent cultural traditions and social organization of the various countries could fail to be deeply impressed by the difficulties in finding a common approach to many human problems. The growing tension preceding the Second World War accentuated these difficulties and created many barriers to free intercourse between nations. Nevertheless, international scientific co-operation continued as a decisive factor in the development which, shortly before the outbreak of the war, raised the prospect of releasing atomic energy on a vast scale.

The fear of being left behind was a strong incentive in various countries to explore, in secrecy, the possibilities of using such energy sources for military purposes. The joint American-British project remained unknown to me until, after my escape from occupied Denmark in the autumn of 1943, I came to England at the invitation of the British government. At that time I was taken into confidence about the great enterprise which had already then reached an advanced stage.

Everyone associated with the atomic energy project was, of course, conscious of the serious problems which would confront humanity once the enterprise was accomplished. Quite apart from the role atomic weapons might come to play in the war, it was clear that permanent grave dangers to world security would ensue unless measures to prevent abuse of the new formidable means of destruction could be universally agreed upon and carried out.

As regards this crucial problem, it appeared to me that the very necessity of a concerted effort to forestall such ominous threats to civilization would offer quite unique opportunities to bridge international divergences. Above all, early consultations between the nations allied in the war about the best ways jointly to obtain future security might contribute decisively to that atmosphere of mutual confidence which would be essential for co-operation on the many other matters of common concern.

In the beginning of 1944, I was given the opportunity to bring such views to the attention of the American and British governments. It may be in the interest of international understanding to record some of the ideas which at that time were the object of serious deliberation. For this purpose, I may quote from a memorandum which I submitted to President Roosevelt as a basis for a long conversation which he granted me in August 1944 [. . .]

> It certainly surpasses the imagination of anyone to survey the consequences of the project in years to come, where in the long run the enormous energy sources which will be available may be expected to revolutionize industry and transport. The fact of immediate preponderance is, however, that a weapon of an unparalleled power is being created which will completely change all future conditions of warfare.
>
> Quite apart from the question of how soon the weapon will be ready for use and what role it may play in the present war, this situation raises a number of problems which call for most urgent attention. Unless, indeed, some agreement about the control of the use of the new active materials can be obtained in due time, any temporary advantage, however great, may be outweighed by a perpetual menace to human security.
>
> Ever since the possibilities of releasing atomic energy on a vast scale came in sight, much thought has naturally been given to the question of control, but the further the exploration of the scientific problems concerned is proceeding, the clearer it becomes that no kind of customary measures will suffice for this purpose and that especially the terrifying prospect of a future competition between nations about a weapon of such formidable character can only be avoided through a universal agreement in true confidence.
>
> In this connection it is above all significant that the enterprise, immense as it is, has still proved far smaller

than might have been anticipated and that the progress of the work has continually revealed new possibilities for facilitating the production of the active materials and of intensifying their effects.

The prevention of a competition prepared in secrecy will therefore demand such concessions regarding exchange of information and openness about industrial efforts including military preparations as would hardly be conceivable unless at the same time all partners were assured of a compensating guarantee of common security against dangers of unprecedented acuteness.

The establishment of effective control measures will of course involve intricate technical and administrative problems, but the main point of the argument is that the accomplishment of the project would not only seem to necessitate but should also, due to the urgency of mutual confidence, facilitate a new approach to the problems of international relationship.

The present moment where almost all nations are entangled in a deadly struggle for freedom and humanity might at first sight seem most unsuited for any committing arrangement concerning the project. Not only have the aggressive powers still great military strength, although their original plans of world domination have been frustrated and it seems certain that they must ultimately surrender, but even when this happens, the nations united against aggression may face grave causes of disagreement due to conflicting attitudes towards social and economic problems [. . .]

The secrecy regarding the project which prevented public knowledge and open discussion of a matter so profoundly affecting international affairs added, of course, to the complexity of the task of the statesmen. With full appreciation of the extraordinary character of the decisions which the proposed initiative involved, it still appeared to me that great opportunities would be lost unless the problems raised by the atomic development were incorporated into the plans of the allied nations for the post-war world.

This viewpoint was elaborated in a supplementary memorandum in which also the technical problem of control measures was further discussed. In particular, I attempted to stress that just the mutual openness, which now was obviously necessary for common security, would in itself promote international understanding and pave the way for enduring co-operation. This memorandum, dated March 24th 1945, contains, besides remarks which have no interest to-day, the following passages:

> Above all, it should be appreciated that we are faced only with the beginning of a development and that, probably within the very near future, means will be found to simplify the methods of production of the active substances and intensify their effects to an extent which may permit any nation possessing great industrial resources to command powers of destruction surpassing all previous imagination.
>
> Humanity will, therefore, be confronted with dangers of unprecedented character unless, in due time, measures can be taken to forestall a disastrous competition in such formidable armaments and to establish an international control of the manufacture and use of the powerful materials.

Any arrangement which can offer safety against secret preparations for the mastery of the new means of destruction would, as stressed in the memorandum, demand extraordinary measures. In fact, not only would universal access to full information about scientific discoveries be necessary, but every major technical enterprise, industrial as well as military, would have to be open to international control. [. . .]

Looking back on those days, I find it difficult to convey with sufficient vividness the fervent hopes that the progress of science might initiate a new era of harmonious co-operation between nations, and the anxieties lest any opportunity to promote such a development be forfeited.

Until the end of the war I endeavoured by every way open to a scientist to stress the importance of appreciating the full political implications of the project and to advocate that, before there could be any question of use of atomic weapons, international co-operation be initiated on the elimination of the new menaces to world security [. . .]

When the war ended and the great menaces of oppression to so many peoples had disappeared, an immense relief was felt all over the world. Nevertheless, the political situation was fraught with ominous forebodings. Divergences in outlook between the victorious nations inevitably aggravated controversial matters arising in connection with peace settlements. Contrary to the hopes for future fruitful co-operation, expressed from all sides and embodied in the Charter of the United Nations, the lack of mutual confidence soon became evident.

The creation of new barriers, restricting the free flow of information between countries, further increased distrust and anxiety. In the field of science, especially in the domain of atomic physics, the continued secrecy and restrictions deemed necessary for security reasons hampered international co-operation to an extent which split the world community of scientists into separate camps. [. . .]

I turn to the United Nations with these considerations in the hope that they may contribute to the search for a realistic approach to the grave and urgent problems confronting humanity. The arguments presented suggest that every initiative from any side towards the removal of obstacles for free mutual information and intercourse would be of the greatest importance in breaking the present deadlock and encouraging others to take steps in the same direction. The efforts of all supporters of international co-operation, individuals as well as nations, will be needed to create in all countries an opinion to voice, with ever increasing clarity and strength, the demand for an open world.

June 9, 1950

29

Lillian Hellman's Letter to the House Un-American Activities Committee on the Fifth Amendment, 1952

The author Mary McCarthy once remarked of Lillian Hellman that that 'every word she writes is a lie, including "and" and "the"'. Hellman was, nevertheless, a hugely successful Broadway playwright before the age of thirty and went on to become a well-remunerated Hollywood screenwriter. A committed leftist (and by some accounts an apologist for Stalinist terrors), she counted Dorothy Parker as an intimate friend and Dashiell Hammett as a long-term lover. Ever economical with the truth, she did, however, take the defiantly principled stance of refusing to name names when called upon to appear before the House Un-American Activities Committee (HUAC), which was little more than a witch-hunt, orchestrated by Senator Joseph McCarthy, against those in Hollywood who were suspected to hold left-wing sympathies. Hellman pleaded the Fifth Amendment protection against self-incrimination and was subsequently blacklisted.

May 19, 1952

Dear Mr Wood:

As you know, I am under subpoena to appear before your committee on May 21, 1952.

I am most willing to answer all questions about myself. I have nothing to hide from your committee and there is nothing in my life of which I am ashamed. I have been advised by counsel that under the fifth amendment I have a constitutional privilege to decline to answer any questions about my political opinions, activities, and associations, on the grounds of self-incrimination. I do not wish to claim this privilege. I am ready and willing to testify before the representatives of our Government as to my own opinions and my own actions, regardless of any risks or consequences to myself.

But I am advised by counsel that if I answer the committee's questions about myself, I must also answer questions about other people and that if I refuse to do so, I can be cited for contempt. My counsel tells me that if I answer questions about myself, I will have waived my rights under the fifth amendment and could be forced legally to answer questions about others. This is very difficult for a layman to understand. But there is one principle that I do understand: I am not willing, now or in the future, to bring bad trouble to people who, in my past association with them, were completely innocent of any talk or any action that was disloyal or subversive. I do not like subversion or disloyalty in any form and if I had ever seen any I would have considered it my duty to have reported it to the proper authorities. But to hurt innocent people whom I knew many years ago in order to save myself is, to me, inhuman and indecent and dishonorable. I cannot and will not cut my conscience to fit this year's fashions, even though I long ago came to the conclusion that I was not a political person and could have no comfortable place in any political group.

I was raised in an old-fashioned American tradition and there were certain homely things that were taught to me: To try to tell the truth, not to bear false witness, not to harm my neighbor, to be loyal to my country, and so on. In general, I respected these ideals of Christian honor and did as well with them as I knew how. It is my belief that you will agree with these simple rules of human decency and will not expect me to violate the good American tradition from which they spring. I would, therefore, like to come before you and speak of myself.

I am prepared to waive the privilege against self-incrimination and to tell you everything you wish to know about my views or actions if your committee will agree to refrain from asking me to name other people. If the committee is unwilling to give me this assurance, I will be forced to plead the privilege of the fifth amendment at the hearing.

A reply to this letter would be appreciated.

Sincerely yours,
Lillian Hellman

30

Paul Robeson's Open Letter to Jackie Robinson on Civil Rights, 1953

Born in Princeton, New Jersey in 1898, the son of a former plantation slave-turned-pastor, Paul Robeson was an actor, singer, athlete, cultural scholar, author and political activist. He spent time in London in the late 1920s, where he joined hunger marches with striking miners from the Rhondda Valley, and visited the USSR several times throughout the 1930s, as well as travelling to the front lines of the Spanish Civil War. On his return to America after the Second World War, his left-wing views put him at odds with Senator Joseph McCarthy's campaign to cleanse the entertainment industry of communists.

In 1949, Jackie Robinson, the African-American baseball star who played for the Brooklyn Dodgers, accepted an invitation by the House Un-American Activities Committee (HUAC) to testify against Robeson. Robinson was a Second World War veteran and a liberal Republican who disagreed with Robeson's support for the Soviet Union, and felt that civil rights could best be advanced by the Republican Party. Nevertheless, he was uneasy about being pitted against another African-American celebrity; his criticisms, in an era of paranoid Cold War rhetoric about 'reds under beds', were restrained, and towards the end of his life, he confessed that he regretted the appearance. Robeson, respectful of Robinson's right to hold differing opinions and believing they had much in common, sought to build bridges between them, while also educating the fellow-sportsman. In 1953, in response to a magazine interview in which Robinson had been asked about his view on civil rights in sport, Robeson issued this open letter, calling on him to be more outspoken on the issue.

April 1953

I notice in a recent issue of *Our World* magazine that some folks think you're too outspoken. Certainly not many of our folks share that view. They think like you that the Yankees, making many a "buck" out of Harlem, might have had a few of our ball players just like Brooklyn. In fact I know you've seen where a couple of real brave fellows, the Turgerson brothers, think it's about time we continued our breaking into the Southern leagues – Arkansas and Mississippi included.

I am happy, Jackie, to have been in the fight for real democracy in sports years ago. I was proud to stand with Judge Landis in 1946 and, at his invitation, address the major league owners, demanding that the bars against Negroes in baseball be dropped. I knew from my experiences as a pro football player that the fans would not only take us – but like us. That's now been proven many times over.

Maybe these protests around you, Jackie, explain a lot of things about people trying to shut up those of us who speak out in many other fields.

You read in the paper every day about "doings" in Africa. These things are very important to us. A free Africa – a continent of 200 millions of folks like us and related to us – can do a lot to change things here.

In South Africa black folks are challenging Malan, a kind of super Ku Kluxer. These Africans are refusing to obey Jim Crow laws. They want some freedom like we do, and they're willing to suffer and sacrifice for it. Malan and a lot of powerful American investors would like to shut them up and lock them up.

Well, I'm very proud that these African brothers and sisters of ours play my records as they march in their parades. A good part of my time is spent in the work of the Council on African Affairs, supervised by Dr. Alphaeus Hunton, an expert on Africa and son of a great YMCA leader, the late William Hunton. Co-chairman of the Council is Dr. W.E.B. Du Bois, one of the greatest Americans who ever lived. We raise funds for Africans and bring information to Americans about the conditions in Africa – conditions to be compared with, but worse than, those in Mississippi and Alabama.

We bring the truth about Kenya, for example – about a man like Kenyatta, leader of the Kikiyu, a proud African people of centuries of culture. I know Kenyatta. He's a highly educated man, with many more degrees than we have, Jackie. He's getting seven years in jail because he wants his people to be free. And there are Americans of African descent who are today on trial, in jail, fugitives, or dead (!) because they fought in their own way for their people to be free. Kenyatta's sentence calls to mind Ben Davis, Henry Winston, James Jackson, Claudia Jones, Pettis Perry and, yes, Harry Moore.

What goes here, Jackie? Well, I'll tell you. The same kind of people who don't want you to point up injustices to your folks, the same people who think you ought to stay in your "place," the same people who want to shut you up – want to shut up any one of us who speaks out for our full equality, for all of our rights.

That's the heart of what I said in Paris in 1949, for example. As a matter of fact the night before I got to Paris 2,000 representatives of colored colonial peoples from all over the world (most of them students in English universities) asked me and Dr. Dadoo, leader of the Indian population in South Africa, to greet the Congress of Peace in Paris in their name.

These future leaders of their countries were from Nigeria, Gold Coast, South Africa, Kenya, Java, Indonesia, India, Jamaica, Trinidad, Barbados, the Philippines, Japan, Burma, and other lands. They were the shapers of the future in the Eastern and colonial world and they asked us to say to this Congress representing about 800 million of the world's 2,000 million that they and their countries wanted peace, no war with anybody. They said they certainly did not want war with the Soviet Union and China because these countries had come out of conditions similar to their own. But the Soviet Union and China were now free of the so-called "free western" imperialist powers. They were countries which had proved that colonial countries could get free, that colored peoples were as good as any other.

All these students made it clear that they felt that the nations who wanted war wanted it in order to head off struggles of colonial peoples, as in Indo-China, Malaya, Africa and Korea, for freedom. For example, if you could start a war in Africa the authorities could clamp down completely with war measures. (It's bad enough now!)

The students felt that peace was absolutely needed in order for their peoples to progress. And certainly, they said they saw no need to die for foreign firms which had come in and taken their land, rubber, cocoa, gold, diamonds, copper and other riches.

And I had to agree that it seemed to me that the same held good in these United States. There was and is no need to talk of war against any nation. We Afro-Americans need peace to continue the struggle for our full rights. And there is no need for any of our American youth to be used as cannon and bomb fodder anywhere in the world.

So I was and am for an immediate ceasefire in Korea and for peace. And it seemed and still seems unthinkable to me that colored or working folk anywhere would continue to rush to die for these who own most of the stocks and bonds, under the guise of false patriotism.

I was born and raised in America, Jackie – on the East Coast as you were on the West. I'm a product of American institutions, as you. My father was a slave and my folks worked cotton and tobacco, and still do in Eastern North Carolina. I'll always have the right to speak out, yes, shout at the top of my voice for full freedom for my people here, in the West Indies, in Africa – and for our real allies, actual and potential, millions of poor white workers who will never be free until we are free.

And, Jackie, the success of a few of us is no final answer. It helps, but this alone can't free all of us. Your child, my grandchildren, won't be free until our millions, especially in the South, have full opportunity and full human dignity.

We fight in many ways. From my experience, I think it's got to be a militant fight. One has to square off with the enemy once in a while.

Thanks for the recognition that I am a great ex-athlete. In the recent record books the All-American team of 1918 and the nationally-picked team of 1917 have only ten players – my name is omitted.

And also thanks for the expression of your opinion that I'm certainly a great singer and actor. A lot of people in the world think so and would like to hear me. But I can't get a passport. And here in my own America millions of Americans would like to hear me. But I can't get auditoriums to sing or act in. And I'm sometimes picketed by the American Legion and other Jim Crow outfits. I have some records on the market but have difficulty getting shops to take them.

People who "beef" at those of us who speak out, Jackie, are afraid of us. Well, let them be afraid. I'm continuing to speak out, and I hope you will, too. And our folks and many others like them all over the world will make it – and soon!

Believe me, Jackie.

Yours
Paul Robeson

31

Rachel Carson's Letter to the *Washington Post* on the Natural World, 1953

In her most famous book, *Silent Spring*, published in 1962, Rachel Carson issued an irrefutable warning about the dangers to the environment caused by the widespread use of pesticides like DDT. A nature writer and 'ecologist' before the term had even been coined, Carson prophetically questioned the effects of humans on the natural environment. She worked as a marine biologist for the US Fish and Wildlife Service in Washington, DC while writing her first book, *Under the Sea-Wind*, which was published in 1941. Her second, a biography of the ocean entitled *The Sea Around Us*, appeared in 1951 and became an international bestseller. Such was its success that Carson was even asked to provide the liner notes to a recording of Debussy's *La Mer* by Arturo Toscanini.

The Republicans won the White House in 1952 and began reorganising many government departments along more pro-business lines. Albert M. Day, the director of the Fish and Wildlife Service, who had both a solid scientific background and a strong belief in wildlife conservation, was replaced with a non-professional, political appointee, John L. Farley. In the wake of this, Carson wrote to the *Washington Post* to protest at what she believed was an alarming development that would inevitably have consequences for the natural world.

22 April 1953

The dismissal of Mr. Albert M. Day as director of the Fish and Wildlife Service is the most recent of a series of events that should be deeply disturbing to every thoughtful citizen. The ominous pattern that is clearly being revealed is the elimination from the Government of career men of long experience and high professional competence and their replacement by political appointees [. . .]

The real wealth of the Nation lies in the resources of the earth – soil, water, forests, minerals, and wildlife. To utilize them for present needs while insuring their preservation for future generations requires a delicately balanced and continuing program, based on the most extensive research. Their administration is not properly, and cannot be, a matter of politics.

By long tradition, the agencies responsible for these resources have been directed by men of professional stature and experience, who have understood, respected, and been guided by the findings of their scientists [. . .]

For many years public-spirited citizens throughout the country have been working for the conservation of the natural resources, realizing their vital importance to the Nation. Apparently their hard-won progress is to be wiped out, as a politically minded Administration returns us to the dark ages of unrestrained exploitation and destruction.

It is one of those ironies of our time that, while concentrating on the defense of our country against enemies from without, we should be so heedless of those who destroy it from within.

32

Czesław Miłosz's Open Letter to Pablo Picasso on Communism, 1956

Having lived in Tsarist Russia, under Nazi occupation in Poland, and then during Soviet-supported communist rule, Czesław Miłosz had a deep understanding of authoritarianism. The Lithuanian-born Polish poet, novelist, essayist, memoirist and winner of the 1980 Nobel Prize for Literature was briefly a member of the Polish communist government's diplomatic service, but defected to the West in 1951.

On 25 February 1956, Nikita Khrushchev used his address at the Twentieth Congress of the Communist Party of the Soviet Union to deliver an astonishing denunciation of Joseph Stalin. For four solid hours, Khrushchev delivered a litany of the former Soviet leader's crimes that stunned delegates into complete silence. From the execution, torture and imprisonment of loyal party members to failures in agricultural policies that had led to mass starvation on a horrifying scale, the world was soon left in no doubt as to the extent of the atrocities perpetrated under the iron rule of 'Uncle Joe'.

Picasso had joined the French Communist Party shortly after the liberation of Paris in 1944. In 1950 the artist was awarded the Stalin Peace Prize for designing the emblem of the Soviet-supported Mouvement de la Paix, while on Stalin's death three years later, he painted a portrait of him as a young man; ironically, this picture was denounced by the leadership of the French Communist Party for not doing 'justice to the moral, spiritual, and intellectual personality of Stalin'.

Despite Khrushchev's criticism and the emergence of further revelations about the regime, Picasso continued to support the party financially. Miłosz's letter was originally published in June 1956 in the French anti-communist magazine *Preuves* which, like its UK near-contemporary *Encounter*, received financial support from the CIA. The letter's appearance in English in *Dissent* magazine followed brutal Soviet repression of Hungary's liberalising government that autumn, which only added weight to the poet's criticism of the painter's unflagging support for the despotic regime.

Dissent Magazine, Autumn 1956

This open letter to Picasso originally appeared in the June 1956 issue of _Preuves_

This letter to you, Picasso, is not a personal letter. You are a genius, hence a part of our human commonwealth in the same way as beautiful structures of past ages, the paintings of the Louvre, or the sound of music transmitted through the centuries. That you are alive among us is only an accident thanks to your fine constitution and the resistance of your arteries which have allowed you to reach a venerable age. It was also a providential accident that you did not belong to one of those racial or national groups destined to be destroyed, along with their potential Picassos.

Your achievement has transformed you into a symbol, but your preference for white or red wine, or for rare or well-done meat will quickly be forgotten. Nonetheless, you share our passions and our errors. Like each of us you are responsible for what happens on our planet and your particular responsibility is measured by the distance between your renown and the anonymity of ordinary citizens.

During the years when painting was systematically being destroyed in the USSR and the "people's democracies," you lent your name to manifestos glorifying the regime of Stalin. At the same time, you scoffed at "socialist realism," thereby proving that certain artistic methods are valid only where the arm of the police is long enough. You were right to take advantage of your privilege, but you seem to forget that is all it was! If there exists a solidarity between men for whom beauty is more than a subject of esthetic considerations, you refused it. But are you absolutely sure that, because of this refusal, you did not rob some young painter of the joy contained in a life of creative fulfillment? Or are you absolutely sure that geniuses are born only in civilized countries and not among the barbarians east of the Elbe?

Let me give you an example. In 1948, while I was in the United States as a cultural attaché for the Polish "People's Democracy", I prepared an exhibition of gouaches painted by young children of my country. They were wonders of boldness and naïve imagination; all the exuberance of pure color was in them. A year later all the children attending this art school were subjected to what was called ideological education. They were to be changed into ten year old adults, to portray in dull and drab colors tractors and May Day parades.

I need hardly tell you what your name, quite appropriately annexed by the Stalinists, has been used to cover up. Almost all that needs to be known about this is now being said in the East. Since you are unacquainted with the Central and Eastern European languages, I will translate a few passages for you.

In the spring of 1956 a Warsaw writer wrote the following:

> The history of philosophy knows few eras in which intolerance was pushed so far as during these past few years. The persecution of critical thought at the beginning of the Renaissance and later on in the 17th and 18th centuries appears almost idyllic when compared with the time through which we have lived and which, we can say with relief, is on its way out.

An eminent poet of Warsaw has told of his experiences.

> In 1949 or 1950 I remember an editor deleting the word "love" from one of my poems on the grounds that, "It is not love, but hate that we preach." And to intimidate me, he added that I might be suspected of deviation because of this![. . .]

Another writer declared, "We are guilty of lying," and he asks himself:

> Were we really so cut off from all information about the deprivations and crimes of the period just passed that now, like those Germans who, after the arrival of the Allied troops, calmly said, "Auschwitz? We never heard of it until you told us about it," we have the right to say the same?

Now imagine, Picasso, your biography containing the following passage: "At the height of Hitler's power, Picasso painted his portrait!" You did Stalin's portrait and it provoked the Party's disapproval because it did not conform to the rules of photographic resemblance. You had dared to attempt more: to bring out the leader's soul, a fine fellow filled with love for humanity. Do you realize the ridiculousness of this? If you answer us by saying, "After all, Stalin wasn't that bad," you deny the testimony published in the press of the East by people who know of what they write.

For years I have been carrying within me the story of a human heart; a story entrusted to me in deepest secrecy. I can tell it to you now, Picasso, because the person in question can now speak aloud. She is a Russian woman, of a goodness and purity whose quality is rarely found among other peoples. She once lived in Moscow, where she studied at the University and worked in a state enterprise. She had married a young Communist whom she loved very much. A child was born to them. Just at that moment – it was 1937 – her husband was arrested and disappeared into the dark void of the concentration camp. She herself – please note this – could count on nobody's pity or help. She even had to pretend that nothing had happened and to appear each morning at her office, smiling and satisfied! For had they known about her hustand's arrest, they would have thrown her out – and there was the child. Then followed year after year of vain hope. It doesn't matter when and where I met her; somewhere in Eastern Europe. All she knew was that her husband was alive, in a camp near the Polar circle. Count her days and nights, multiply them by 8, 10, 15 millions of similar human story and you will know to what political use you have been putting your glory as a painter!

[. . .] But even a short time ago, in the political circles surrounding you, each denunciation of the Stalin regime was branded as the work of forgers, traitors and reactionaries. Or else 'historical necessity' was invoked. Now, you can, if you like, say I am motivated by a natural villainy; but the evidence will not change. As for 'historical necessity', what's left of it if it served as a mask to the aberration who nearly handed Russia over to Hitler.

I accuse you, Picasso, and not only you, but all the artists and intellectuals of the West who let themselves be trapped by words. In that period of cruelties and sufferings, all of you, free as you were to choose, chose the most prudent conformism. It gave you – perhaps also your conscience – an air of men belonging to the side of progress. But in fact, your weight added to the balance and deprived of all hope, those in the East who did not want to submit to the absurd. No one can say what would have been the consequence of a categorical protest voiced by all of you against the official doctrine imposed upon art, or against the Rajk trial. If the support you gave to terror counted, then your indignation would also have counted. It is therefore just that your irresponsibility be pointed out so that your future biographers may not forget it.

It is one of those ironies of our time that, while concentrating on the defense of our country against enemies from without, we should be so heedless of those who destroy it from within.

Rachel Carson

33

Doris Lessing's Letter to E.P. Thompson on the Communist Party, 1957

Raised in Southern Rhodesia (now Zimbabwe), the writer and novelist Doris Lessing had rebelled against the stifling atmosphere of her British colonial upbringing and joined the Southern Rhodesia Communist Party in the 1940s. She arrived in Britain in 1950 with the manuscript of her first novel, *The Grass is Singing*, and soon joined the Communist Party of Great Britain. Although she was dismayed by the revelations about the crimes committed under Stalin. Following the brutal suppression of Hungary's reform-minded government in November 1956, when Soviet tanks had roamed the streets of Budapest, picking off demonstrators, Lessing resigned from the party. She nevertheless remained politically active: her denunciation of apartheid and racism during a tour of South Africa and Rhodesia resulted in her ban from both countries, and she attended the first public meeting of what would become the Campaign for Nuclear Disarmament (CND) and took part in the first Aldermaston anti-nuclear march in 1958.

Reflecting on this period in her second autobiography she wrote:

> We talk about the invasion of Hungary, but this has become, with the passing of time, the event people remember now. For us, living through all that, Hungary was the culmination of a series of ugly events, one being the Soviet suppression of the uprising in East Berlin in – I think – 1953.

In this letter to her friend, the historian E.P. Thompson, she writes about her break with the party and her renewed belief in the power of art to respond to events and transform the world.

---

58 Warwick Road
London SW5
21 Feb 1957

My dear Edward,

I think autobiography is a good idea. A really truthful bit of writing about experience in the C.P. at some stormy point would be invaluable, but I shall be very surprised if people are ready to be truthful writers or readers. The instinctive defence against being truthful is so very strong.

I think it would be interesting to have a serious description by someone like Kingsley Amis of his experience with the C.P.* It would be typical of the experience of hundreds of thousands of people *vis a vis* the C.P. But these angry young men have nothing philosophically to utter. Why would they have? They are all artists not philosophers [. . .]

[F]or my recent novel, *Retreat to Innocence*, I think it was a bad book, because I wasn't facing up to any essential issue – I wasn't being truthful with myself, although I imagined I was, and so it's soft-centred and sentimental. I don't hold with it. Though it's got some good bits in it.†

But what I am trying to say is more complicated than all this:

Look, when I read your letters I feel as if you were reaching out for some kind of final word or statement from me; as if you wanted something of me, and I ask myself, why? And what is it?

But above all our moods are very different.

I know full well that all my reactions now are because (if I may use this word I hate so much) I am an artist, and I've

---

* Kingsley Amis was never a member of the Communist Party.

† Lessing later suppressed *Retreat to Innocence* refusing to allow it to be republished after the 1960s and never including it in lists of her published works.

exhausted all the experience and emotions that are useful to me as an artist in the old way of being a communist [. . .]

I shall wither and die and never write another word if I can't get out of this straitjacket of what we've all been thinking and feeling for so long.

But this is not a political attitude, and this is why I don't think you ought to ask for clarification.

And I suspect you of being an artist, in which case you ought to be finding out what you think by writing it [. . .]

You have been a pure and high-minded communist, and until recently wouldn't accept the evil in it, and your idealism is hurt and your picture of yourself is damaged.

Get thee to thy typewriter, dear Edward. You can communicate your experience in art, and as such it can be communicated. But what have your lost feelings got to do with philosophies?

We are living in a time, I am convinced, when there aren't likely to be any philosophies to pay allegiance to. Marxism is no longer a philosophy but a system of government, differing from country to country.

Which is a good thing. Any philosophy which lasts longer than fifty years must be a bad one, because everything changes so fast.

I know I am a socialist and I believe in the necessity for revolution when the moment is opportune. But whether the economists like Ken and John, or the historians are right as Marxists, I don't know. How could one know? It seems to me that a great many of the concepts we have called Marxist are simply the relocation of the pressures of the time we live in.

I don't want to make any more concepts. For myself, I mean.

I want to let myself simmer into some sort of knowledge, but I don't know what it is.

Do you think there is something to be said for the point of view of being a communist has never been (except for a very few people) a question of intellectual standpoint, but rather a sort of sharing of moral fervour?

I haven't any moral fervour left. No one who feels responsible for the bloodbaths and cynicism of the last thirty years can feel morally indignant about the bloodymindedness of capitalism?

I can't anyway.

What I feel is an immense joy and satisfaction that the world is going so far, that the peasants in China no longer starve, that people all over the world care enough for their fellow human beings to fight for what they feel, at the time, to be justice. I feel a sort of complicated gigantic flow of movement of which I am a part, and it gives me profound satisfaction to be in it. But what has this got to do with political attitudes?

I want to write a lot of books.

And the stale aroma of thirty years of dead political words makes me feel sick.

I know quite well, since you are looking for something from me, this letter will make you feel let down. But I can't help it.

You shouldn't go asking people like me for certainties.

I feel as though I have been let out of prison.

But above all I am convinced you should get yourself in front of a typewriter and ask yourself what you think.

Love Doris

34

Tony Dyson et al.'s Letter to *The Times* on Homosexuality, 1958

Homosexual acts between men were made illegal in Britain in 1885, under the Criminal Law Amendment Act. By the 1950s, over a thousand men each year were being imprisoned because of their sexuality. In 1954, the issue hit the headlines when three aristocratic young men, Lord Montagu of Beaulieu, his cousin Michael Pitt-Rivers and his friend Peter Wildeblood, were convicted, on the evidence of two RAF servicemen, of 'performing "gross offences"' and of 'conspiracy to incite certain male persons to commit serious offences with male persons'. In the aftermath of this trial, a government committee was convened to look into the laws around homosexuality and prostitution, chaired by Sir John Wolfenden, the Vice-Chancellor of the University of Reading. His report was published in September 1957 and recommended 'that homosexual acts between two consenting adults should no longer be a criminal offence'.

Tony Dyson was an academic and literary critic who had known he was gay since his teens. While Wolfenden advised him against a public campaign in support of homosexual rights, Dyson pressed on and obtained the signatures of such luminaries as Clement Attlee, Isaiah Berlin and J.B. Priestley, for a letter he sent to *The Times*.

A debate on the report was held in parliament, but a motion to implement its findings in 1960 was lost and a further seven years would elapse before homosexuality was finally decriminalised.

HOMOSEXUAL ACTS – CALL TO REFORM THE LAW

7 March 1958

TO THE EDITOR OF THE TIMES

Sir, – We, the undersigned, would like to express our general agreement with the recommendation of the Wolfenden Report that homosexual acts committed in private between consenting adults should no longer be a criminal offence.

The present law is clearly no longer representative of either Christian or liberal opinion in this country, and now that there are widespread doubts about both its justice and its efficacy, we believe that its continued enforcement will do more harm than the good to the health of the community as a whole.

The case for reform has already been accepted by most of the responsible papers and journals, by two Archbishops, the Church Assembly, a Roman Catholic committee, a number of non-conformist spokesmen, and many other organs of informed public opinion.

In view of this, and of the conclusions which the Wolfenden Committee itself agreed upon after a prolonged study of evidence, we should like to see the Government introduce legislation to give effect to the proposed reform at an early date; and are confident that if that does so it will deserve the widest support from humane men of all parties.

Yours, & c.,
N.G. ANNAN; ATTLEE; A.J. AYER; ISAIAH BERLIN; LEONARD BIRMINGHAM †; ROBERT BOOTHBY; C.M. BOWRA; C.D. BROAD; DAVID CECIL; L. JOHN COLLINS; ALEX COMFORT; A.E. DYSON; ROBERT EXON †: GEOFFREY FABER; JACQUETTA HAWKES; TREVOR HUDDLESTON, C.R.; JULIAN HUXLEY; C. DAY LEWIS; W.R. NIBLETT; J.B. PRIESTLEY; RUSSELL; DONALD O. SOPER; STEPHEN SPENDER; MARY STOCKS; A.J.P. TAYLOR; E.M.W. TILL-YARD; ALEC R. VIDLER; KENNETH WALKER; LESLIE D. WEATHERHEAD; C.V. WEDGWOOD; ANGUS WILSON; JOHN WISDOM; BARBARA WOOTTON.

35

Alan Paton et al.'s Open Letter to Harold Macmillan on Apartheid, 1959

In 1948, D.F. Malan's National Party had swept into power in South Africa and immediately set about extending existing policies of racial segregation, under a system it called 'Apartheid'. Its chief architect was the white Afrikaner nationalist, Dr Hendrik Verwoerd, who served as the Minister of Native Affairs in Malan's first administration and succeeded him as Prime Minister in 1958. Verwoerd reaffirmed his commitment to apartheid with further legislation, and in 1959 the Extension of University Education Act brought wholesale segregation to tertiary education. But opposition to apartheid was growing both at home and abroad. On the eve of Harold Macmillan's state visit to South Africa, a group of anti-apartheid campaigners, including the white South African novelist Alan Paton, sent an open letter to the *Observer*, calling on the Prime Minister not to show any sign of support for this unjust regime.

As it was, Macmillan, who in his memoirs recalled that 'even in small matters' Verwoerd 'pressed apartheid to the extreme', spoke out against South Africa's racial policies in the famous 'Winds of Change' speech, which he delivered to the all-white South African parliament in Cape Town, on 3 February 1960.

South African Plea to Macmillan

20 December 1959

We do not expect, Sir, that while you are the guest of our Government, you will publicly criticise their policies, under which the name of *apartheid* have become everywhere notorious, to an extent which our rulers begin to find alarming. We would not ask you to do this, though such a speech would ring throughout the world. It would shorten the life of these policies by twenty-five years and bring new hope to those who suffer under the colour bar, the hope that freedom, fully expected for their children, might even be miraculously be known by them also.

We make an earnest plea to you of quite another kind, not that you will criticise *apartheid*, but that you will not say one single word that could be construed to be in praise of it.

You will find it extraordinarily difficult to do this, and we would not ask you to do it if we did not think that you are a man who knows the world, and be simultaneously urbane and resolute. And you will need to be all the more careful because we have recently suffered a visit from Field-Marshal Viscount Montgomery, who, after a tour the superficiality of which would be impossible to equal, has returned to Britain with the highest regard for our Prime Minister, a man who would cheerfully have seen the annihilation of Montgomery and the whole British Army, the defeat of the Commonwealth and its allies, and the triumph of Hitler and his barbarian policies of racial superiority.

The Field-Marshal was the guest here of Sir Francis de Guingand, who heads a new organisation known as the South Africa Foundation, which has received much influential business support, and which was launched, according to Sir Francis, 'to present the other side of the case.' Sir Francis stated in London in August that he resented the one-sided way in which South African affairs were reported abroad.

The Field-Marshal has therefore left behind him in South Africa the unpleasant impression that he came out here in the interests of certain business men, and that these business men, concerned about the growing isolation of South Africa and therefore about their business interests, wanted the Field-Marshal to return to England 'to present the other side of the case', which means, in brief, 'the better side of *apartheid*.'

As far as we are concerned, honoured Sir, *apartheid* has no better side; it is evil and unjust, and contemptuous of persons. It now goes under the name of *separate development*, and it is by holding up the dream of complete separation, each group having its own territory, its own institutions, its own autonomy, that our rulers have succeeded in seducing some people who ought to have known better.

Separate development is only *apartheid* in a new dress and it means fundamentally the rejection of one's fellow-countrymen and their segregation in poor, inferior, subordinate societies.

African freehold owners are going to be deprived of the land which meant for them freedom from the narrow life of the reserves and farms. The threat of removal hangs over all the Indian business men of South Africa; already the decree has gone out that the Indian traders of Johannesburg must move to a point twenty miles from the city. Professor Z.K. Matthews, at the end of a long and honourable life, must give up his work and his pension because he cannot accept the new university rules which will not permit him, among other things, to criticise *apartheid*.

A citizen of Cape Town has just committed suicide because he has been ordered to give up his home under the Group Area Act. A white family is split asunder because the father is discovered, as the result of 'information received', to have coloured ancestry and bitterest irony, not only does his white wife flee from him, but also his children who are now themselves coloured. An African woman, mother of eleven children, is banned without warning to a desolate part of the country.

There, Sir, are the costs of *separate development*, and one cannot help supposing that Viscount Montgomery knew about them, and with that shallow realism which seems to be his chief intellectual characteristic, reflected that one cannot make an omelette without breaking eggs, and thought that the extensive housing schemes of the Government in some way compensated for the harshness of their racial policies.

This, Sir, places on you a great responsibility, as one of the senior leaders of the Commonwealth, and as the representative of a country whose reputation still stands high in South Africa.

It would be the final disillusion if you were to express or imply any approval of our Government's policies, and such approval would confront the Commonwealth with far greater problems that that of retaining the unwilling membership of a country whose

Government keeps her a member only because of the narrowest self-interest of the ruling racial group, masquerading under the title, itself dubious, of 'South Africa First.'

Signed
CHIEF ALBERT LUTHULI, President General of the African National Congress, who is confined under a banishment order;
MR. ALAN PATON, author of *Cry, the Beloved Country* and President of the S.A. Liberal Party;
MR. JORDAN K. NGUBANE, an African journalist and vice-president of the S.A. Liberal Party;
MR G.M. NAICKER, President of the S.A. Indian Congress.

36

W.E.B. Du Bois's Letter to the Communist Party on the Failure of Capitalism, 1961

Born only three years after the abolition of slavery in America, William Edward Burghart 'W.E.B.' Du Bois was the first African-American to earn a doctorate from Harvard University. An academic, socialist, historian, economist, political thinker, pioneering civil rights activist and founding officer of the National Association for the Advancement of Colored People (NAACP), he was also a prolific and versatile author, whose prodigious output ranged from biographies to epic historical novels, but whose towering achievement remains *The Souls of Black Folk* (1903), a book acclaimed in its day as 'the political bible of the Negro race'.

At the age of ninety-three, amidst a period of anti-Soviet Cold War hysteria, Du Bois requested to join the Communist Party, having come to the conclusion that it was the only party that could best represent the needs of the African-American people.

1 October 1961
To Gus Hall, Chairman
Communist Party of the U.S.A.
New York, New York:

On this First day of October, 1961, I am applying for admission to membership in the Communist Party of the United States. I have been long and slow in coming to this conclusion, but at last my mind is settled.

In college I heard the name of Karl Marx, but read none of his works, nor heard them explained. At the University of Berlin, I heard much of those thinkers who had definitively answered the theories of Marx, but again we did not study what Marx himself had said. Nevertheless, I attended meetings of the Socialist Party and considered myself a Socialist.

On my return to America, I taught and studied for sixteen years. I explained the theory of Socialism and studied the organized social life of American Negroes; but still I neither read nor heard much of Marxism. [. . .]

For the next twenty years I tried to develop a political way of life for myself and my people. I attacked the Democrats and Republicans for monopoly and disfranchisement of Negroes; I attacked the Socialists for trying to segregate Southern Negro members; I praised the racial attitudes of the Communites, but opposed [. . .] their advocacy of a Negro state. At the same time I began to study Karl Marx and the Communists; I read *Das Kapital* and other Communist literature; I hailed the Russian Revolution of 1917, but was puzzled at the contradictory news from Russia.

Finally in 1926, I began a new effort: I visited Communist lands. [. . .]

I was early convinced that Socialism was an excellent way of life, but I thought it might be reached by various methods. For Russia I was convinced she had chosen the only way open to her at the time. I saw Scandinavia choosing a different method, half-way between Socialism and Capitalism. In the United States I saw Consumers Cooperation as a path from Capitalism to Socialism, while England, France and Germany developed in the same direction in their own way. After the depression and the Second World War, I was disillusioned. The Progressive movement in the United States failed. The Cold War started. Capitalism called Communism a crime.

Today I have reached a firm conclusion:

Capitalism cannot reform itself; it is doomed to self-destruction. No universal selfishness can bring social good to all.

Communism – the effort to give all men what they need and

to ask of each the best they can contribute – this is the only way of human life. It is a difficult and hard end to reach – it has and will make mistakes, but today it marches triumphantly on in education and science, in home and food, with increased freedom of thought and deliverance from dogma. [. . .]

I will call for:

1. Public ownership of natural resources and of all capital
2. Public control of transportation and communications
3. Abolition of poverty and limitation of personal income
4. No exploitation of labor
5. Social medicine, with hospitalization and care of the old
6. Free education for all
7. Training for jobs and jobs for all
8. Discipline for growth and reform
9. Freedom under law
10. No dogmatic religion.

These aims are not crimes. They are practised increasingly over the world. No nation calls itself free which does not allow its citizens to work for these ends.

W.E.B. Du Bois

37

Nikita Khrushchev's Letter to John F. Kennedy on the Cuban Missile Crisis, 1962

In bringing the United States and the Soviet Union to within a whisker of an all-out nuclear war, the Cuban Missile Crisis of 1962 remains an event that is indelibly etched into the history of the Cold War era.

After Fidel Castro's overthrowal of President Fulgencio Batista's authoritarian rule in 1959, Cuba, a Latin-American island scarcely a hundred miles south of the Florida coast, had been run as a socialist republic with the support of the Soviet Union. Unhappy to have a USSR-aided communist state on their own doorstep, the United States government advanced various schemes to depose Castro. In the spring of 1961, President John F. Kennedy gave his approval to the CIA-orchestrated Bay of Pigs Invasion, which ended in abject failure. Having been long expecting an American invasion along these lines, Castro and the Soviet leader, Nikita Khrushchev, had reached a secret agreement to site Soviet nuclear missiles in Cuba to act as a deterrent.

On 14 October 1962, the pilot of an American U-2 spy plane flying over Cuba photographed a Soviet missile being assembled, and news of this development was relayed to Kennedy. With possible responses ranging from bombing the missile site to an all-out invasion of Cuba, the American President, after much agonising with his advisors, opted for a naval blockage, or quarantine, to stop further missile parts from reaching the island. After terse exchanges, such as the one here sent by Khrushchev to Kennedy on 24 October 1962, a compromise was finally reached four days later. The Soviets agreed to remove their missiles in exchange for America promising to abandon any future attempts to invade Cuba and to withdraw the nuclear arms it had placed in Turkey.

Moscow, October 24, 1962

Dear Mr. President,

Imagine, Mr. President, what if we were to present to you such an ultimatum as you have presented to us by your actions. How would you react to it? I think you would be outraged at such a move on our part. And this we would understand.

Having presented these conditions to us, Mr. President, you have thrown down the gauntlet. Who asked you to do this? By what right have you done this? Our ties with the Republic of Cuba, as well as our relations with other nations, regardless of their political system, concern only the two countries between which these relations exist. And, if it were a matter of quarantine as mentioned in your letter, then, as is customary in international practice, it can be established only by states agreeing between themselves, and not by some third party. Quarantines exist, for example, on agricultural goods and products. However, in this case we are not talking about quarantines, but rather about much more serious matters, and you yourself understand this.

You, Mr. President, are not declaring a quarantine, but rather issuing an ultimatum, and you are threatening that if we do not obey your orders, you will then use force. Think about what you are saying! And you want to persuade me to agree to this! What does it mean to agree to these demands? It would mean for us to conduct our relations with other countries not by reason, but by yielding to tyranny. You are not appealing to reason; you want to intimidate us.

No, Mr. President, I cannot agree to this, and I think that deep inside, you will admit that I am right. I am convinced that if you were in my place you would do the same [. . .]

This Organization [of American States] has no authority or grounds whatsoever to pass resolutions like those of which you speak in your letter. Therefore, we do not accept these resolutions. International law exists, generally accepted standards of conduct exist. We firmly adhere to the principles of international law and strictly observe the standards regulating navigation on the open sea, in international waters. We observe these standards and enjoy the rights recognized by all nations.

You want to force us to renounce the rights enjoyed by every sovereign state; you are attempting to legislate questions of international law; you are violating the generally accepted standards of this law. All this is due not only to hatred for the Cuban people and their government, but also for reasons having to do with the election campaign in the USA. What morals, what laws can justify such an approach by the American government to international affairs? Such morals and laws are not to be found, because the actions of the USA in relation to Cuba are outright piracy. This, if you will, is the madness of a degenerating imperialism. Unfortunately, people of all nations, and not least the American people themselves, could suffer heavily from madness such as this, since with the appearance of modern types of weapons, the USA has completely lost its former inaccessibility.

Therefore, Mr. President, if you weigh the present situation with a cool head without giving way to passion, you will understand that the Soviet Union cannot afford not to decline the despotic demands of the USA. When you lay conditions such as these before us, try to put yourself in our situation and consider how the USA would react to such conditions. I have no doubt that if anyone attempted to dictate similar conditions to you – the USA, you would reject such an attempt. And we likewise say – no.

The Soviet government considers the violation of the freedom of navigation in international waters and air space to constitute an act of aggression propelling humankind into the abyss of a world nuclear-missile war. Therefore, the Soviet government cannot instruct captains of Soviet ships bound for Cuba to observe orders of American naval forces blockading this island. Our instructions to Soviet sailors are to observe strictly the generally accepted standards of navigation in international waters and not retreat one step from them. And, if the American side violates these rights, it must be aware of the responsibility it will bear for this act. To be sure, we will not remain mere observers of pirate actions by American ships in the open sea. We will then be forced on our part to take those measures we deem necessary and sufficient to defend our rights. To this end we have all that is necessary.

Respectfully,
N. Khrushchev

38

Martin Luther King Jr's 'Letter from a Birmingham Jail', 1963

In the spring of 1963, the campaign for African-American civil rights became focused on Birmingham, Alabama. Situated in a southern state with deeply entrenched racist politics, the city was described by Dr Martin Luther King Jr as 'a symbol of hardcore resistance to integration' and was nicknamed 'Bombington' by other activists, because of the violence dished out to those who sought to desegregate the city. That May, the city's infamous Commissioner of Public Safety Bull Connor, set dogs and fire hoses on a 3,000-strong protest primarily composed of school children and students.

The civil rights campaign in Birmingham was organised by the Southern Christian Leadership Conference (SCLC) and spearheaded by King, the Reverend James Bevel and Fred Shuttlesworth. It comprised a series of peaceful protests, sit-ins, boycotts and marches against segregation, to which the local police force responded with outright aggression.

The city authorities duly obtained an injunction, which prohibited public civil rights demonstrations. But King and a few others felt that they needed to breach this injunction to advance their cause, even if it meant risking incarceration. He and the Reverend Ralph Abernathy were arrested on 12 April, Good Friday, and were taken to the city's jail. There, after reading a statement condemning his actions written by a group of eight white local clergymen and published in the *Birmingham News*, he composed what became his 'Letter from a Birmingham Jail' in the margins of the newspaper. The result was one of the most important written documents of the civil rights era.

April 16, 1963

My Dear Fellow Clergymen,

While confined here in the Birmingham City Jail, I came across your recent statement calling our present activities "unwise and untimely." Seldom, if ever, do I pause to answer criticism of my work and ideas [. . .] But since I feel that you are men of genuine good will and your criticisms are sincerely set forth, I would like to answer your statement in what I hope will be patient and reasonable terms.

I think I should give the reason for my being in Birmingham, since you have been influenced by the argument of "outsiders coming in." I have the honor of serving as president of the Southern Christian Leadership Conference, an organization operating in every Southern state with headquarters in Atlanta, Georgia. We have some eighty-five affiliate organizations all across the South. [. . .] Several months ago our local affiliate here in Birmingham invited us to be on call to engage in a nonviolent direct action program if such were deemed necessary. We readily consented. [. . .]

Beyond this, I am in Birmingham because injustice is here. Just as the eighth century prophets left their villages and carried their "thus saith the Lord" far beyond the boundaries of their home towns, and just as the Apostle Paul left his village of Tarsus and carried the gospel of Jesus Christ to practically every hamlet and city of the Greco-Roman world, I too am compelled to carry the gospel of freedom beyond my particular home town. Like Paul, I must constantly respond to the Macedonian call for aid.

Moreover, I am cognizant of the interrelatedness of all communities and states. I cannot sit idly by in Atlanta and not be concerned about what happens in Birmingham. Injustice anywhere is a threat to justice everywhere. We are caught in an inescapable network of mutuality, tied in a single garment of destiny. Whatever affects one directly, affects all indirectly. Never again can we afford to live with the narrow, provincial "outside agitator" idea. Anyone who lives inside the United States can never be considered an outsider anywhere in this country. [. . .]

In any nonviolent campaign there are four basic steps: 1) Collection of the facts to determine whether injustices are alive; 2) Negotiation; 3) Self-purification; and 4) Direct action. We have gone through all of these steps in Birmingham [. . .] Birmingham is probably the most thoroughly segregated city in the United States. Its ugly record of police brutality is known in every section of the country. Its unjust treatment of Negroes in the courts is a notorious reality. There have been more unsolved bombings of Negro homes and churches in Birmingham than in any city in this nation. These are the hard, brutal, and unbelievable facts. On the basis of these conditions Negro leaders sought to negotiate with the city fathers. But the political leaders consistently refused to engage in good faith negotiation.

Then came the opportunity last September to talk with some of the leaders of the economic community. In these negotiating sessions certain promises were made by the merchants – such as the promise to remove the humiliating racial signs from the stores. On the basis of these promises Reverend Shuttlesworth and the leaders of the Alabama Christian Movement for Human Rights agreed to call a moratorium on any type of demonstrations. As the weeks and months unfolded we realized that we were the victims of a broken promise. The signs remained. Like so many experiences in the past, we were confronted with blasted hopes, and the dark shadow of a deep disappointment settled upon us. So we had no alternative except that of preparing for direct action, whereby we would present our very bodies as a means of laying our case before the conscience of the local and national community. We were not unmindful of the difficulties involved. So we decided to go through the process of self-purification. We started having workshops on nonviolence and repeatedly asked ourselves the questions, "Are you able to accept the blows without retaliating?" "Are you able to endure the ordeals of jail?" [. . .]

You may well ask, "Why direct action? Why sit-ins, marches, etc.? Isn't negotiation a better path?" You are exactly right in your call for negotiation. Indeed, this is the purpose of direct action. Nonviolent direct action seeks to create such a crisis and establish such creative tension that a community that has constantly refused to negotiate is forced to confront the issue [. . .] Just as Socrates felt that it was necessary to create a tension in the mind so that individuals could rise from the bondage of myths and half-truths to the unfettered realm of creative analysis and objective appraisal, we must we see the need for nonviolent gadflies to create the kind of tension in society that will help men rise from the dark depths of prejudice and racism to the majestic heights of understanding and brotherhood. [. . .]

My friends, I must say to you that we have not made a single gain in civil rights without legal and nonviolent pressure. History is the long and tragic story of the fact that privileged groups seldom give up their privileges voluntarily. Individuals may see the moral light and give up their unjust posture; but as Reinhold Niebuhr has reminded us, groups are more immoral than individuals.

We know through painful experience that freedom is never voluntarily given by the oppressor; it must be demanded by the oppressed. Frankly I have never yet engaged in a direct action movement that was "well timed," according to the timetable of those who have not suffered unduly from the disease of segregation. For years now I have heard the word "Wait!" It rings in the ear of every Negro with a piercing familiarity. This "Wait" has almost always meant "never." It has been a tranquilizing thalidomide, relieving the emotional stress for a moment, only to give birth to an ill-formed infant of frustration. We must come to see with the distinguished jurist of yesterday that "justice too long delayed is justice denied." We have waited for more than three hundred and forty years for our constitutional and God-given rights. The nations of Asia and Africa are moving with jet-like speed toward the goal of political independence, and we still creep at horse and buggy pace toward the gaining of a cup of coffee at a lunch counter. I guess it is easy for those who have never felt the stinging darts of segregation to say, "Wait." But when you have seen vicious mobs lynch your mothers and fathers at will and drown your sisters and brothers at whim; when you have seen hate-filled policemen curse, kick, brutalize, and even kill your black brothers and sisters with impunity; when you see the vast majority of your twenty million Negro brothers smothering in an airtight cage of poverty in the midst of an affluent society; when you suddenly find your tongue twisted and your speech stammering as you seek to explain to your six-year-old daughter why she can't go to the public amusement park that has just been advertised on television, and see the tears welling up in her little eyes when she is told that Funtown is closed to colored children, and see the depressing clouds of inferiority begin to form in her little mental sky, and see her begin to distort her little personality by unconsciously developing a bitterness toward white people; when you have to concoct an answer for a five-year-old son who is asking in agonizing pathos: "Daddy, why do white people treat colored people so mean?"; when you take a cross country drive and find it necessary to sleep night after night in the uncomfortable corners of your automobile because no motel will accept you; when you are humiliated day in and day out by nagging signs reading "white" men and "colored" when your first name becomes "nigger" and your middle name becomes "boy" (however old you are) and your last name becomes "John," and when your wife and mother are never given the respected title of "Mrs"; when you are harried by day and haunted by night by the fact that you are a Negro, living constantly at tip-toe stance, never quite knowing what to expect next, and plagued with inner fears and outer resentments; when you are forever fighting a degenerating sense of "nobodiness" – then you will understand why we find it difficult to wait. There comes a time when the cup of endurance runs over, and men are no longer willing to be plunged into an abyss of injustice where they experience the bleakness of corroding despair. I hope, Sirs, you can understand our legitimate and unavoidable impatience.

You express a great deal of anxiety over our willingness to break laws. This is certainly a legitimate concern. Since we so diligently urge people to obey the Supreme Court's decision of 1954 outlawing segregation in the public schools, it is rather strange and paradoxical to find us consciously breaking laws. One may well ask, "how can you advocate breaking some laws and obeying others?" The answer lies in the fact that there are two types of laws: There are <u>just</u> and <u>unjust</u> laws. I would agree with St. Augustine that "An unjust law is no law at all."

Now, what is the difference between the two? How does one determine whether a law is just or unjust? A just law is a man-made code that squares with the moral law or the law of God. An unjust law is a code that is out of harmony with the moral law. To put it in the terms of Saint Thomas Aquinas, an unjust law is a human law that is not rooted in eternal law and natural law. Any law that uplifts human personality is just. Any law that degrades human personality is unjust. All segregation statutes are unjust because segregation distorts the soul and damages the personality. It gives the segregator a false sense of superiority, and the segregated a false sense of inferiority. To use the words of Martin Buber, the great Jewish philosopher, segregation substitutes an "I-it" relationship for an "I-thou" relationship and ends up relegating persons to the status of things. Hence segregation is not only politically, economically and sociologically unsound, it is morally wrong and sinful. [. . .]

I hope you are able to see the distinction I am trying to point out. In no sense do I advocate evading or defying the law, as would the rabid segregationist. That would lead to anarchy. One who breaks an unjust law must do so <u>openly</u>, <u>lovingly</u>, (not hatefully as the white mothers did in New Orleans when they were seen on television screaming "nigger, nigger, nigger") and with a willingness to accept the penalty. I submit that an individual who breaks a law that conscience tells him is unjust and willingly accepts the penalty by staying in jail to arouse the conscience of the community over its injustice, is in reality expressing the highest respect for law.

Of course, there is nothing new about this kind of civil disobedience. It was practiced superbly in the refusal of Shadrach, Meshach and Abednego to obey the laws of Nebuchadnezzar, because a higher moral law was involved. It was practiced superbly by the early Christians, who were willing to face hungry lions and the excruciating pain of chopping blocks rather than submit to certain unjust laws of the Roman Empire. To a degree, academic freedom is a reality today because Socrates practiced civil disobedience.

We should never forget that everything Adolf Hitler did in Germany was "legal" and everything the Hungarian freedom fighters did in Hungary was "illegal." It was "illegal" to aid and comfort a Jew in Hitler's Germany. But I am sure that if I lived in Germany during that time, I would have aided and comforted my Jewish brothers, even though it was illegal. If I lived in a communist country today where certain principles dear to the Christian faith are suppressed, I would openly advocate disobeying these anti-religious laws.

I must make two honest confessions to you, my Christian and Jewish brothers. First, I must confess that over the last few years I have been gravely disappointed with the white moderate. I have almost reached the regrettable conclusion that the Negro's great stumbling block in the stride toward freedom is not the White Citizens' "Councilor" or the Ku Klux Klanner, but the white moderate who is more devoted to "order" than to justice; who prefers a negative peace which is the absence of tension to a positive peace which is the presence of justice; who constantly says "I agree with you in the goal you seek, but I can't agree with your methods of direct action;" who paternistically feels that he can set the time-table for another man's freedom; who lives by the myth of time and who constantly advises the Negro to wait until a "more convenient season." Shallow understanding from people of good will is more frustrating than absolute misunderstanding from people of ill will. Lukewarm acceptance is much more bewildering than outright rejection. [. . .]

You spoke of our activity in Birmingham as extreme. At first I was rather disappointed that fellow clergymen would see my nonviolent efforts as those of an extremist. I started thinking about the fact that I stand in the middle of two opposing forces in the Negro community. One is a force of complacency made up of Negroes who, as a result of long years of oppression, have been so completely drained of self-respect and a sense of "somebodiness" that they have adjusted to segregation, and, of a few Negroes in the middle class who, because of a degree of academic and economic security, and because at points they profit from segregation, have unconsciously become insensitive to the problems of the masses. The other force is one of bitterness, and hatred and becomes perilously close to advocating violence. It is expressed in the various black nationalist groups that are springing up over the nation, the largest and best known being Elijah Muhammad's Muslim movement. This movement is nourished by the contemporary frustration over the continued existence of racial discrimination. It is made up of people who have lost faith in America, who have absolutely repudiated Christianity, and who have concluded that the white man is an incurable "devil." [. . .]

The Negro has many pent-up resentments and latent frustrations. He has to get them out. So let him march sometime; let him have his prayer pilgrimages to the city hall; understand why he must have sit-ins and freedom rides. If his repressed emotions do not come out in these nonviolent ways, they will come out in ominous expressions of violence. This is not a threat; it is a fact of history. So I have not said to my people, "Get rid of your discontent." But I have tried to say that this normal and healthy discontent can be channelized through the creative outlet of nonviolent direct action. [. . .]

In spite of my shattered dreams of the past, I came to Birmingham with the hope that the white religious leadership of this community would see the justice of our cause and, with deep moral concern, serve as the channel through which our just grievances could get to the power structure. I had hoped that each of you would understand. But again I have been disappointed.

I have heard numerous religious leaders of the South call upon their worshippers to comply with a desegregation decision because it is the law, but I have longed to hear white ministers say, "follow this decree because integration is morally right and the Negro is your brother." In the midst of blatant injustices inflicted upon the Negro, I have watched white churches stand on the sideline and merely mouth pious irrelevancies and sanctimonious trivialities. In the midst of a mighty struggle to rid our nation of racial and economic injustice, I have heard so many ministers say, "those are social issues with which the Gospel has no real concern," and I have watched so many churches commit themselves to a completely other-worldly religion which made a strange distinction between body and soul, the sacred and the secular. [. . .]

I hope this letter finds you strong in the faith. I also hope that circumstances will soon make it possible for me to meet each of you, not as an integrationist or a civil rights leader, but as a fellow clergyman and a Christian brother. Let us all hope that the dark clouds of racial prejudice will soon pass away and the deep fog of misunderstanding will be lifted from our fear-drenched communities and in some not too distant tomorrow the radiant stars of love and brotherhood will shine over our great nation with all of their scintillating beauty.

Yours for the cause of Peace and Brotherhood,
Martin Luther King, Jr.

I accuse you, Picasso, and not only you, but all the artists and intellectuals of the West who let themselves be trapped by words. In that period of cruelties and sufferings, all of you, free as you were to choose, chose the most prudent conformism.

Czesław Miłosz

39

Joan Baez's Open Letter to the Internal Revenue Service on the Vietnam War, 1964

The folk singer and political activist Joan Baez expressed her committed opposition to the Vietnam War in song, at rallies and in humanitarian visits to Hanoi. But in 1964, aged twenty-three, she issued an open letter to the Internal Revenue Service announcing her intention to withhold the percentage of her taxes she calculated the American government had devoted to military spending.

It was a position of principle, and one she clung on to for a decade. But, as she confessed in her autobiography, *And a Voice to Sing With*, in the end 'the government got my money plus fines'.

April 1964

Dear Friends

What I have to say is this:

I do not believe in war.

I do not believe in the weapons of war.

Weapons and war have murdered, burned, distorted, crippled, and caused endless varieties of pain to men, women, and children for too long. Our modern weapons can reduce a man to a piece of dust in a split second, can make a woman's hair to fall out or cause her baby to be born a monster. They can kill the part of a turtle's brain that tells him where he is going, so, instead of trudging to the ocean, he trudges confusedly toward the desert, slowly blinking his poor eyes until he finally scorches to death and turns into a shell and some bones.

I am not going to volunteer the 60% of my year's income tax that goes to armaments. There are two reasons for my action. One is enough. It is enough to say that no man has the right to take another man's life. Now we plan and build weapons that can take thousands of lives in a second, millions of lives in a day, billions in a week.

No one has the right to do that.

It is madness.

It is wrong.

My other reason is that modern war is impractical and stupid. We spend billions of dollars a year on weapons which scientists, politicians, military men, and even presidents all agree must never be used. That is impractical. The expression "National Security" has no meaning. It refers to our Defense System, which I call our Offense System, and which is a farce. It continues expanding, heaping up, one horrible kill machine upon another until, for some reason or another, a button will be pushed and our world, or a good portion of it, will be blown to pieces. That is not security. That is stupidity.

People are starving to death in some places of the world. They look to this country with its wealth and all its power. They look at our national budget. They are supposed to respect us. They do not respect us. They despise us. That is impractical and stupid.

Maybe the line should have been drawn when the bow and arrow were invented, maybe the gun, the cannon, maybe. Because now it is all wrong, all impractical, and all stupid.

So all I can do is draw my own line. I am no longer supporting my portion of the arms race . . .

Sincerely yours,
Joan C. Baez

40

Ernesto 'Che' Guevara's Letter to Fidel Castro on Leaving Cuba, 1965

Ernesto Guevara de la Serna, better known as 'Che' Guevara, was born into an affluent middle-class family in Rosario, Argentina. He studied medicine at the University of Buenos Aires but in 1952 he undertook a motorcycle journey across South America that opened his eyes to the continent's widespread poverty and political inequality. Two years later, he met Fidel and Raúl Castro in Mexico and subsequently joined their revolution in Cuba, leading guerrilla troops in battle against the Caribbean country's authoritarian, US-backed Batista regime. Guevara would go on to serve as Cuba's Minister of Industry and the president of her national bank. But, convinced that the ideas of revolution needed to be exported elsewhere, he left there in 1965, sending this farewell letter to Castro.

He ended up in Bolivia, where his call to arms received a rather more muted response, and he was killed by the Bolivian Army in 1967.

Havana
April 1, 1965.

Fidel:

At this moment I remember many things: when I met you in Maria Antonia's house, when you proposed I come along, all the tensions involved in the preparations. One day they came by and asked who should be notified in case of death, and the real possibility of it struck us all. Later we knew it was true, that in a revolution one wins or dies (if it is a real one). Many comrades fell along the way to victory.

Today everything has a less dramatic tone, because we are more mature, but the event repeats itself. I feel that I have fulfilled the part of my duty that tied me to the Cuban revolution in its territory, and I say farewell to you, to the comrades, to your people, who now are mine.

I formally resign my positions in the leadership of the party, my post as minister, my rank of commander, and my Cuban citizenship. Nothing legal binds me to Cuba. The only ties are of another nature – those that cannot be broken as can appointments to posts.

Reviewing my past life, I believe I have worked with sufficient integrity and dedication to consolidate the revolutionary triumph. My only serious failing was not having had more confidence in you from the first moments in the Sierra Maestra, and not having understood quickly enough your qualities as a leader and a revolutionary.

I have lived magnificent days, and at your side I felt the pride of belonging to our people in the brilliant yet sad days of the Caribbean [Missile] crisis. Seldom has a statesman been more brilliant as you were in those days. I am also proud of having followed you without hesitation, of having identified with your way of thinking and of seeing and appraising dangers and principles.

Other nations of the world summon my modest efforts of assistance. I can do that which is denied you due to your responsibility as the head of Cuba, and the time has come for us to part.

You should know that I do so with a mixture of joy and sorrow. I leave here the purest of my hopes as a builder and the dearest of those I hold dear. And I leave a people who received me as a son. That wounds a part of my spirit. I carry to new battlefronts the faith that you taught me, the revolutionary spirit of my people, the feeling of fulfilling the most sacred of duties: to fight against imperialism wherever it may be. This is a source of strength, and more than heals the deepest of wounds.

I state once more that I free Cuba from all responsibility, except that which stems from its example. If my final hour finds me under other skies, my last thought will be of this people and especially of you. I am grateful for your teaching and your example, to which I shall try to be faithful up to the final consequences of my acts.

I have always been identified with the foreign policy of our revolution, and I continue to be. Wherever I am, I will feel the responsibility of being a Cuban revolutionary, and I shall behave as such. I am not sorry that I leave nothing material to my wife and children; I am happy it is that way. I ask nothing for them, as the state will provide them with enough to live on and receive an education.

I would have many things to say to you and to our people, but I feel they are unnecessary. Words cannot express what I would like them to, and there is no point in scribbling pages.

41

John Steinbeck's Letter to Ernest Heyn on the Exploration of the Seas, 1966

John Steinbeck, the author of such classic twentieth-century American novels as *The Grapes of Wrath* and *Of Mice and Men*, grew up in reasonable comfort in Salinas in California, a mere hamlet of 3,000 people. Witnessing both its transformation by money-grabbing developers and the after-effects of the Great Depression on the wider Californian region had a profound effect on him. As the foremost chronicler in the fiction of the Dust Bowl migration, Steinbeck took an acute interest in environmental issues.

Confounded by the American government's expenditure on space exploration he issued this letter to Ernest Heyn, the editor of *Popular Science*, calling for the establishment of a NASA for the oceans, which appeared in the September 1966 issue of the magazine.

September 1966

Dear Ernie Heyn:

I know enough about the sea to know how pitifully little we know about it. We have not, as a nation and a world, been alert to the absolute necessity of going back to the sea for our survival.

I do not think $21 billion, or a hundred of the same, is too high a price for a round-trip ticket to the moon. But it does seem unrealistic, unreasonable, romantic, and very human that we indulge in these passionate pyrotechnics when, under the seas, three-fifths of our own world and over three-fifths of our world's treasure is unknown, undiscovered, and unclaimed.

Please believe, Ernie, that my passion for the world's seas and underseas does not lessen my interest in our space probes. When the astronauts go up in their beautiful skyrockets, my stomach goes up with them until it collides with my lungs and pushes them against my throat. I set my clock for two a.m. recently to watch a crazy scarecrow-like structure settle gently on the moon, a job of such intricacy as to stagger the imagination. But besides the sweetness and delicacy of the thinking, planning, and building, the very fact that we do it proves that human beings have not changed – we are still incurable, incorrigible romantics.

We may think back with wonder on people capable of a search for the Golden Fleece, capable of picking up their lives and going on crusade in the Middle Ages – but are we any different? The budget for getting two Americans on the moon is $21 billion, and it will necessarily come to much more. And what they will bring back will be what Dr. Urey calls a pocketful of rocks for him to analyze. If you ask an American why we want to get to the moon, he will usually say, "To get there before the Russians," and the Russians probably use the same answer – to get there before we do. Pressed further, the one polled will go off into a burble of pseudoscientific jargon and equally pseudomilitary nonsense. Dr Urey gives a truer reason – because we are curious. And it seems to me that one of the definitive diagnostics of the human animal, besides being the key to his success in survival and triumph over the forces of nature, is curiosity.

But, while the lifeless rubbled surface of the inconstant moon becomes increasingly littered with the burnt-out bones of vehicles, the bathyscaphe has visited the deep and unknown places of the earth only a few times. There is never much argument about appropriations for space shots, but a recent request for money to explore, map, and evaluate the hidden places of our mother earth brought howls of protest from Congressional leaders and the inevitable question – is it really necessary?

Ernie, I'm going to try to put down some of the reasons why I think it is really necessary to explore the sea.

There is something for everyone in the sea . . . food for the hungry . . . incalculable wealth . . . the excitement and danger of exploration . . .

It is a pitiful few thousand years that have passed since men and women roamed the earth eating anything that didn't eat them first. Men moved as the game moved, and the game followed the grass. With the domestication of animals, the roving continued, but only following the grass. With the beginning of agriculture, the crops stood still and most men settled down. But over the years, by selection, the animals changed and the cereals changed.

The grains we use today have little resemblance to their ancestor seeds, and the animals could not be recognized by their early progenitors. Man has changed the face of the earth and the inhabitants thereof, with the possible exception of himself. But the seas he has not changed.

In our relation to three-fifths of the world, we correspond exactly to Neolithic man – fearful, ignorant, and swinish.

We peck like sandpipers along the edges for the small treasures the restless waves wash up. We raid the procession of the migrating fishes, killing all we can. Even the killer whale herds the sperm whales and kills them only when it needs food – but we have wiped out some species entirely. We have not improved nor changed a single species of sea-going fish. And the huge agriculture of the seas we have ignored completely, except to rip out the fringes for iodine or fertilizer.

I said that three-fifths of the earth's surface is under the seas – but, with the washing down from the continents of minerals and chemicals, it is probable that four-fifths of the world's wealth is there.

More important in the near future, the plankton, the basic reservoir of the world's food, live in the sea. We have not even learned to make this boundless bank of protein food available for our bellies.

Of all the mysteries and enigmas of our world, man is the strangest and most incomprehensible. Without the pressure of cold, hunger, disease, danger from outside, and even greater danger from the quarrelsome combativeness in his own heart, it is probable that he would still be living in trees, and still eating everything he could kill or break up into bite-sized chunks.

Survival has been the mother of our inventiveness. War has spawned not only weaponry, but a knowledge of mechanics in all directions. General Hap Arnold once remarked that without war we would probably never have developed the airplane, and between wars development just about ceased.

We have wiped out the animal predators that once decimated embattled families. We are by way of defeating the micro-enemies which secretly invaded our bodies to strike from within. And finally we find ourselves faced with the most ghastly enemy of all – ourselves, too many of us in a world with a limited food supply. And hungry men will destroy anything, even themselves, to get food.

We peck like sandpipers along the edges for the small treasures the restless waves wash up. At the same time we have invented the cold war, a continuing state of hostility between wars, which keeps our inventiveness in the mechanics of destructiveness alive. This, too, may be the result of our uneasiness in the face of our exploding numbers. Meanwhile, the intricate and expensive skyrockets litter space with an orbiting junk pile, and we can easily justify it as a means of defense.

But it is possible that we may be driven back to our mother, the sea, because we are running out of supplies. Two men with their pockets full of moon rocks will not solve the situation. On the other hand, the planning, computing minds which so gently laid that crazy-looking scarecrow on the moon could easily design the means, not only for exploring our watery world, but for placing whole producing cities on the sea bottom.

If our inventive minds were given the money and the incentive of necessity for the desalting and moving of sea water, it would be a very short time before life-giving water would flow to desert places which make up so much of our world, so that they might flower and produce.

To me, personally, the oceans mean safety, mystery, and wonder.

During the depression I lived by the sea and took most of my protein food from it and lived very well indeed.

I have studied the endless variety of ocean animal life – hundreds of thousands more species than are to be found on land.

Several years ago I went along as an observer on the Mohole Project. You remember that was the expedition which put down a drill string to the earth's crust under 18,000 feet of water near Guadalupe Island, off the west coast of Mexico. We didn't get very far – took six cores through sediment and into the basic basalt of the earth's crust. But on the basis of those six cores, textbooks had to be rewritten.

What we found was older than we expected and different from what we thought was there. But an attempt to probe farther has met strong resistance from some money-allotting members of Congress.

The men in the rockets are rather like human sacrifices, taking a part of all of us with them. Oceanology, on the other hand, is slow, undramatic, and singularly unrewarded, although the gifts it can bring to us are measureless and will soon be desperately needed.

Many wonderful men are working, studying, evaluating. At this writing there is a convention in Moscow attended by most of the world's profound students and authorities in oceanography, oceanology, seismology, zoology. They have gathered to discuss and to describe what they have learned, and what they hope to learn.

Experiments are going on all over the world. Cousteau has men living undersea, and so has the American Navy. Men are learning the techniques of changing pressures. Whereas the astronauts must become accustomed to weightlessness and vacuum, the undersea men must learn to endure the opposites. They receive little official encouragement.

What the exploration of the wet world lacks, and must have to proceed, is organization. Undersea study is split up into a thousand unrelated groups, subjects, plans, duplications, having neither direction nor directors. There is no one to establish the path to be followed and see that it is taken. Our space probes could not have gotten off the ground without NASA, a management for analysis, planning, engineering, and coordinating, having the power to give orders and the money to carry them out. The movement to possess the sea must be given the strength and structure to move.

We must explore our world and then we must farm it and harvest its plant life. We must study, control, herd, and improve the breeds of animals, because we are shortly going to need them. And we must mine the minerals, refine the chemicals to our use. Surely the rewards are beyond anything we can now conceive, and will be increasingly needed in an over-populated and depleting world.

There is something for everyone in the sea – incredible beauty for the artist, the excitement and danger of exploration for the brave and restless, an open door for the ingenuity and inventiveness of the clever, a new world for the bored, food for the hungry, and incalculable material wealth for the acquisitive – and all of these in addition to the pure clean wonder of increasing knowledge.

Why, Ernie, even the lawyers will have a field day. No one owns the underseas. Think of the happy thunder of argument over property rights.

For myself, I am hungry for the experience. When the next Mohole expedition goes out, I am going with it. I want to go down in the bathyscaphe to the great black depths. I can't wait. Surely all this should have at least equal backing with space.

Yours,
John Steinbeck

42

Ron Ridenhour's Letter on the My Lai Massacre, 1969

The My Lai massacre was one of the worst single atrocities of the Vietnam War. As many as 500 civilians, including many young women and children, were slaughtered in a killing frenzy by a company of American soldiers in the village of My Lai on 16 March 1968. Many of the women had been raped before being shot, and yet senior US Army officials colluded in covering up the incident. But a young helicopter gunner, Ronald Ridenhour, though not present himself, had heard about the atrocity from fellow soldiers who had witnessed it. Convinced that the perpetrators must be held to account for their crimes, in March 1969 he wrote a letter detailing what he knew about My Lai and sent it to thirty members of Congress and to Pentagon officials, including the President, Richard Nixon.

Its revelations stoked international outrage, but a substantial proportion of Americans initially refused to believe Ridenhour's account or assumed that such killings were simply a factor of war. But once the full truth was established, and the savage brutality of the soldiers' actions known, Ridenhour's letter helped change what the American population thought about a war supposedly being waged in the name of freedom and democracy.

1416 East Thomas Road #104
Phoenix, Arizona
March 29, 1969

Gentlemen:

It was late in April, 1968 that I first heard of "Pinkville" and what allegedly happened there. I received that first report with some skepticism, but in the following months I was to hear similar stories from such a wide variety of people that it became impossible for me to disbelieve that something rather dark and bloody did indeed occur sometime in March, 1968 in a village called "Pinkville" in the Republic of Viet Nam.

The circumstances that led to my having access to the reports I'm about to relate need explanation. I was inducted in March, 1967 into the U.S. Army. After receiving various training I was assigned to the 70th Infantry Detachment (LRP), 11th Light Infantry Brigade at Schofield Barracks, Hawaii, in early October, 1967. That unit, the 70th Infantry Detachment (LRP), was disbanded a week before the 11th Brigade shipped out for Viet Nam on the 5th of December, 1967. All of the men from whom I later heard reports of the "Pinkville" incident were reassigned to "C" Company, lst Battalion, 20th Infantry, 11th Light Infantry Brigade. I was reassigned to the aviation section of Headquarters Company 11th LIB. After we had been in Viet Nam for 3 to 4 months many of the men from the 70th Inf. Det. (LRP) began to transfer into the same unit, "E" Company, 51st Infantry (LRP).

In late April, 1968 I was awaiting orders for a transfer from HHC, 11th Brigade to Company "E," 51st Inf, (LRP), when I happened to run into Pfc "Butch" Gruver, whom I had known in Hawaii. Gruver told me he had been assigned to "C" Company 1st of the 20th until April 1st when he transferred to the unit that I was headed for. During the course of our conversation he told me the first of many reports I was to hear of "Pinkville."

"Charlie" Company 1/20 had been assigned to Task Force Barker in late February, 1968 to help conduct "search and destroy" operations on the Batangan Peninsula, Barker's area of operation. The task force was operating out of L.F. Dottie, located five or six miles north of Quang Nhai city on Viet Namese National Highway 1. Gruver said that Charlie Company had sustained casualties; primarily from mines and booby traps, almost everyday from the first day they arrived on the peninsula. One village area was particularly troublesome and seemed to be infested with booby traps and enemy soldiers. It was located about six miles northeast of Quang Nhai city at approximate coordinates B.S. 728795. It was a notorious area and the men of Task Force Barker had a special name for it: they called it "Pinkville." One morning in the latter part of March, Task Force Barker moved out from its firebase headed for "Pinkville." Its mission: destroy the trouble spot and all of its inhabitants.

When "Butch" told me this I didn't quite believe that what he was telling me was true, but he assured me that it was and went on to describe what had happened. The other two companies that made up the task force cordoned off the village so that "Charlie" Company could move through to destroy the structures and kill the inhabitants. Any villagers who ran from Charlie Company were stopped by the encircling companies. I asked "Butch" several times if all the people were killed. He said that he thought they were men, women and children. He recalled seeing a small boy, about three or four years old, standing by the trail with a gunshot wound in one arm. The boy was clutching his wounded arm with his other hand, while blood trickled between his fingers. He was staring around himself in shock and disbelief at what he saw. "He just stood there with big eyes staring around like he didn't understand; he didn't believe what was happening. Then the captain's RTO (radio operator) put a burst of 16 (M-16 rifle) fire into him." It was so bad, Gruver said, that one of the men in his squad shot himself in the foot in order to be medivaced out of the area so that he would not have to participate in the slaughter. Although he had not seen it, Gruver had been told by people he considered trustworthy that one of the company's officers, 2nd Lieutenant Kally (this spelling may be incorrect) had rounded up several groups of villagers (each group consisting of a minimum of 20 persons of both sexes and all ages). According to the story, Kally then machine-gunned each group. Gruver estimated that the population of the village had been 300 to 400 people and that very few, if any, escaped.

After hearing this account I couldn't quite accept it. Somehow I just couldn't believe that not only had so many young American men participated in such an act of barbarism, but that their officers had ordered it. There were other men in the unit I was soon to be assigned to, "E" Company, 51st Infantry (LRP), who had been in Charlie Company at the time that Gruver alleged the incident at "Pinkville" had occurred. I became determined to ask them about "Pinkville" so that I might compare their accounts with Pfc Gruver's.

When I arrived at "Echo" Company, 51st Infantry (LRP) the first men I looked for were Pfcs Michael Terry, and William Doherty. Both were veterans of "Charlie" Company, 1/20 and "Pinkville." Instead of contradicting "Butch" Gruver's story they corroborated it, adding some tasty tidbits of information of their own. Terry and Doherty had been in the same squad and their platoon was the third platoon of "C" Company to pass through the village. Most of the people they came to were already dead. Those that weren't were sought out and shot. The platoon left nothing alive neither livestock nor people. Around noon the two soldiers' squads stopped to eat. "Billy and I started to get out our chow," Terry said, "but close to us was a bunch of Vietnamese in a heap, and some of them were moaning. Kally (2nd Lt. Kally) had been through before us and all of them had been shot, but many weren't dead. It was obvious that they weren't going to get any medical attention so Billy and I got up and went over to where they were. I guess we sort of finished them off." Terry went on to say that he and Doherty then returned to where their packs were and ate lunch. He estimated the size of the village to be 200 to 300 people. Doherty thought that the population of "Pinkville" had been 400 people.

If Terry, Doherty and Gruver could be believed, then not only had "Charlie" Company received orders to slaughter all the inhabitants of the village, but those orders had come from the commanding officer of Task Force Barker, or possibly even higher in the chain of command. Pfc Terry stated that when Captain Medina (Charlie Company's commanding officer Captain Ernest Medina) issued the order for the destruction of "Pinkville" he had been hesitant, as if it were something he didn't want to do but had to. Others I spoke to concurred with Terry on this.

It was June before I spoke to anyone who had something of significance to add to what I had already been told of the "Pinkville" incident. It was the end of June, 1968 when I ran into Sargent Larry La Croix at the USO in Chu Lai. La Croix had been in 2nd Lt. Kally's platoon on the day Task Force Barker swept through "Pinkville." What he told me verified the stories of the others, but he also had something new to add. He had been a witness to Kally's gunning down at least three separate groups of villagers. "It was terrible. They were slaughtering villagers like so many sheep." Kally's men were dragging people out of bunkers and hootches and putting them together in a group. The people in the group were men, women and children of all ages. As soon as he felt that the group was big enough, Kally ordered a M-60 (machine gun) set up and the people killed. La Croix said that he bore witness to this procedure at least three times. The three groups were of different sizes, one of about twenty people, one of about thirty people and one of about forty people. When the first group was put together Kally ordered Pfc Torres to man the machine-gun and open fire on the villagers that had been grouped together. This Torres did, but before everyone in the group was down he ceased fire and refused to fire again. After ordering Torres to recommence firing several times, Lieutenant Kally took over the M-60 and finished shooting the remaining villagers in that first group himself. Sargent La Croix told me that Kally didn't bother to order anyone to take the machine-gun when the other two groups of villagers were formed. He simply manned it himself and shot down all villagers in both groups.

This account of Sargent La Croix's confirmed the rumors that Gruver, Terry and Doherty had previously told me about Lieutenant Kally. It also convinced me that there was a very substantial amount of truth to the stories that all of these men had told. If I needed more convincing, I was about to receive it.

It was in the middle of November, 1968 just a few weeks before I was to return to the United States for separation from the army that I talked to Pfc Michael Bernhardt. Bernhardt had served his entire year in Viet Nam in "Charlie" Company 1/20 and he too was about to go home. "Bernie" substantiated the tales told by the other men I had talked to in vivid, bloody detail and added this. "Bernie" had absolutely refused to take part in the massacre of the villagers of "Pinkville" that morning and he thought that it was rather strange that the officers of the company had not made an issue of it. But that evening "Medina" (Captain Ernest Medina) came up to me ("Bernie") and told me not to do anything stupid like write my congressman" about what had happened that day. Bernhardt assured Captain Medina that he had no such thing in mind. He had nine months left in Viet Nam and felt that it was dangerous enough just fighting the acknowledged enemy.

Exactly what did, in fact, occur in the village of "Pinkville" in March, 1968 I do not know for *certain*, but I am convinced that it was something very black indeed. I remain irrevocably persuaded that if you and I do truly believe in the principles, of justice and the equality of every man, however humble, before the law, that form the very backbone that this country is founded on, then we must press forward a widespread and public investigation of this matter with all our combined efforts. I think that it was Winston Churchill who once said "A country without a conscience is a country without a soul, and a country without a soul is a country that cannot survive." I feel that I must take some positive action on this matter. I hope that you will launch an investigation immediately and keep me informed of your progress. If you cannot, then I don't know what other course of action to take.

I have considered sending this to newspapers, magazines and broadcasting companies, but I somehow feel that investigation and action by the Congress of the United States is the appropriate procedure, and as a conscientious citizen I have no desire to further besmirch the image of the American serviceman in the eyes of the world. I feel that this action, while probably it would promote attention, would not bring about the constructive actions that the direct actions of the Congress of the United States would.

Sincerely,
Ron Ridenhour

43

Nelson Mandela's Letter to his Daughters on their Mother's Imprisonment, 1969

On 12 June 1964, Nelson Mandela, the South African leader of the banned African National Congress (ANC), was sentenced to life imprisonment on charges of sabotage, treason, violent conspiracy and inciting strikes. Trained as a lawyer, Mandela had offered a stirring defence of his anti-apartheid actions from the dock in the form of a speech, in which he concluded:

> During my lifetime I have dedicated myself to this struggle of the African people. I have fought against white domination, and I have fought against black domination. I have cherished the ideal of a democratic and free society in which all persons live together in harmony and with equal opportunities. It is an ideal which I hope to live for and to achieve. But if needs be, it is an ideal for which I am prepared to die.

The death penalty was a very real possibility for Mandela. While he remained in jail, the fight to end apartheid continued, with his wife, Winnie Madikizela-Mandela, playing an increasingly prominent role in the struggle. Subject to constant police surveillance and harassment, she was herself frequently arrested and imprisoned. The below letter from Nelson to their two daughters Zenani and Zindzi was written in 1969, shortly after Winnie had been detained under Section 6 of a new Terrorism Act, which allowed the security police to hold and interrogate people for as long as they wanted; as a result, she would spend 491 days in jail.

Nelson Mandela was eventually released in 1990, the same year that negotiations to end apartheid began. When South Africa's first multi-racial elections were finally held between 26 and 29 April 1994, the ANC won a historic 62 per cent of the vote, and Mandela was inaugurated as the country's first black President.

---

23 June 1969

My darlings,

Once again our beloved mummy has been arrested and now she and daddy are away in jail. My heart bleeds as I think of her sitting in some police cell far away from home, perhaps alone and without anybody to talk to, and with nothing to read. Twenty-four hours of the day longing for her little ones. It may be many months or even years before you see her again. For long you may live, like orphans, without your own home and parents, without the natural love, affection and protection mummy used to give you. Now you will get no birthday or Christmas parties, no presents or new dresses, no shoes or toys. Gone are the days when, after having a warm bath in the evening, you would sit at table with mummy and enjoy her good and simple food. Gone are the comfortable beds, the warm blankets and clean linen she used to provide. She will not be there to arrange for friends to take you to bioscopes, concerts and plays, or to tell you nice stories in the evening, help you read different books and to answer the many questions you would like to ask. She will be unable to give you the help and guidance you need as you grow older and as new problems arise. Perhaps never again will mummy and daddy join you in House no. 8115 Orlando West, the one place in the whole world that is so dear to our hearts.

This is not the first time mummy goes to jail. In October 1958, only four months after our wedding, she was arrested with 2,000 other women when they protested against passes in Johannesburg and spent two weeks in jail. Last year she served four days, but now she has gone back again and I cannot tell you how long she will be away this time. All that I wish you always to bear in mind is that we have a brave and determined mummy who loves her people with all her heart. She gave up pleasure and comfort in return for a life full of hardship and misery, because of the deep love she has for her people and country. When you become adults and think carefully of the unpleasant experiences mummy has gone through, and the stubbornness with which she has held to her beliefs, you will begin to realise the importance of her contribution in the battle for truth and justice and the extent to which she has sacrificed her own personal interests and happiness [. . .]

44

Václav Havel's Letter to Dr Gustáv Husák on Repression, 1975

Described as 'one of three key players in the death of Soviet communism' by the *Spectator* in 2014, the dissident Czech playwright and philosopher Václav Havel endured long periods in prison, was vilified on state television and saw his works banned.

While welcoming the reforms ushered in by the Czech leader Alexander Dubček during the Prague Spring in 1968 that were intended to create a 'socialism with a human face', Havel called for an end to one-party rule, arguing that communism could never be tamed. When even these modest changes were crushed, with Soviet tanks dispatched to Prague that August and Dubček dismissed from office, Havel continued to press for political freedom.

In 1975 he wrote an open letter to Gustáv Husák, the President of Czechoslovakia, criticising the Government's repressive policy of 'normalisation', a series of steps taken to reverse the progress achieved by Dubček. When Czechoslovakia's Velvet Revolution swept Husák and the communists from power in 1989, Havel was elected his successor in the first free elections in Czechoslovakia since 1946.

Dear Dr Husák

[. . .] If every day someone takes order in silence from an incompetent superior, if every day he solemnly performs ritual acts which he privately finds ridiculous, if he unhesitatingly gives answers to questionnaires which are contrary to his real opinions and is prepared to deny himself in public, if he sees no difficulty in feigning sympathy or even affection where, in fact, he feels only indifference or aversion, it still does not mean that he has entirely lost the use of one of the basic human senses; the sense of dignity.

On the contrary: even if they never speak of it, people have a very acute appreciation of the price they have paid for outward peace and quiet: the permanent humiliation of their human dignity. The less direct resistance they put up to it – comforting themselves by driving it from their mind and deceiving themselves with the thought that it is of no account, or else simply gritting their teeth – the deeper the experience etches itself into their emotional memory. The man who can resist humiliation can quickly forget it; but the man who can long tolerate it must long remember it. In actual fact, then, nothing remains forgotten. All the fear one has endured, the dissimulation one has been forced into, all the painful and degrading buffoonery, and, worst of all perhaps, the feeling of having displayed one's cowardice – all this settles and accumulates somewhere in the bottom of our social consciousness, quietly fermenting. Clearly, this is no healthy situation. Left untreated, the abscesses suppurate; the pus cannot escape from the body and the malady spreads throughout the organism. The natural human emotion [. . .] is gradually deformed into a sick cramp, into a toxic substance not unlike the carbon monoxide produced from incomplete combustion.

No wonder, then, that when the crust cracks and the lava of life rolls out, there appear not only well-considered attempts to rectify old wrongs, not only searchings for truth and for reforms matching life's needs, but also symptoms of bilious hatred, vengeful wrath, and a feverish desire for immediate compensation for all the degradation endured. [. . .]

The Czechs and Slovaks, like any other nation, harbour within themselves simultaneously the most disparate potentialities. We have had, still have, and will continue to have our heroes, and, equally, our informers and traitors. We are capable of unleashing our imagination and creativity, of rising spiritually and morally to unexpected heights, of fighting for the truth and sacrificing ourselves for others.

But it lies in us equally to succumb to total apathy, to take no interest in anything but our bellies, and to spend our time tripping one another up. And though human souls are far from being mere pint pots that anything can be poured into (note the arrogant implications of that dreadful phrase so frequent in official speeches, when it is complained that "we" – that is, "the government" – find that such-and-such ideas are being instilled into people's heads), it depends, nevertheless, very much on the leaders which of these contrary tendencies that slumber in society will be mobilized, which set of potentialities will be given the chance of fulfilment, and which will be suppressed.

So far, it is the worst in us which is being systematically activated and enlarged – egotism, hypocrisy, indifference, cowardice, fear, resignation, and the desire to escape every personal responsibility, regardless of the general consequences.

Yet even today's national leadership has the opportunity to influence society by its policies in such a way as to encourage not the worse side of us, but the better.

So far, you and your government have chosen the easy way out for yourselves, and the most dangerous road for society: the path of inner decay for the sake of outward appearances; of deadening life for the sake of increasing uniformity; of deepening the spiritual and moral crisis of our society, and ceaselessly degrading human dignity, for the puny sake of protecting your own power.

Yet, even within the given limitations, you have the chance to do much toward at least a relative improvement of the situation. This might be a more strenuous and less gratifying way, whose benefits would not be immediately obvious and which would meet with resistance here and there. But in the light of our society's true interests and prospects, this way would be vastly the more meaningful one.

As a citizen of this country, I hereby request, openly and publicly, that you and the leading representatives of the present regime consider seriously the matters to which I have tried to draw your attention, that you assess in their light the degree of your historic responsibility, and act accordingly.

April 1975

45

Red Saunders et al.'s Letter to the Music Press on Racism in Rock Music, 1976

On 5 August 1976, the rock guitarist Eric Clapton, who had recently scored a number one hit with his cover of Bob Marley's reggae classic 'I Shot the Sheriff', took to the stage of the Odeon in Birmingham. By his own admission the worse for drink, Clapton furiously ranted that Britain was becoming 'a black colony' and advised his audience to vote for the right-wing Conservative MP Enoch Powell, to 'get the foreigners out' and 'keep Britain white'. Powell's incendiary 'Rivers of Blood' speech, calling for the repatriation of non-whites, had been delivered just a few miles away eight years earlier. Since then, the far right National Front party had made considerable gains across the country, and there appeared to be a rising tide of racism, which was encapsulated in Clapton's poisonous remarks.

The photographer Red Saunders wrote the below letter to decry his comments and suggest the creation of a grass roots movement to fight rascism in music. He then phoned round friends to ask them to sign it and sent it in to the *New Musical Express*, *Melody Maker*, *Sounds* and the *Socialist Worker*. The result was Rock Against Racism: a series of groundbreaking multi-racial gigs and festivals which sought to celebrate diversity and boasted performances from the likes of Tom Robinson, the Clash, Misty in Roots and the Specials.

28 August 1976

When I read about Eric Clapton's Birmingham concert when he urged support for Enoch Powell, we nearly puked.

What's going on, Eric? You've got a touch of brain damage. So you're going to stand for MP and you think we're being colonized by black people. Come on . . . you've been taking too much of that *Daily Express* stuff, you know you can't handle it.

Own up, half your music is black. You're rock music's biggest colonist. You're a good musician but where would you be without the blues and R&B?

You've got to fight the racist poison, otherwise you degenerate into the sewer with the rats and all the money men who ripped off rock culture with their chequebooks and plastic crap.

Rock was and still can be a real progressive culture, not a package mail-order stick-on nightmare of mediocre garbage.

We want to organize a rank-and-file movement against the racist poison in rock music – we urge support – all those interested please write to: ROCK AGAINST RACISM, Box M, 8 Cotton Gardens, London E2 8DN

PS. 'Who shot the sheriff,' Eric? It sure as hell wasn't you!

Signed: Peter Bruno, Angela Follett, Red Saunders, Jo Wreford, Dave Courts, Roger Huddle, Mike Stadler, etc.

I am begging you to resist the pressures of pragmatism, of money, of the oily cowardice of diplomats and to stand up resolutely and proudly for humanity the world over, as your movement is *pledged* to do.

Stephen Fry

46

Armistead Maupin's 'Letter to Mama' on Coming Out, 1977

In 1974 Armistead Maupin began to write a regular column for the *Pacific Sun* newspaper; a contemporary fictional serial in the mode of Dickens, it was based on the lives of people he knew around the Castro district of San Francisco. In the aftermath of the 'peace and love' hippie movement in the city's Haight-Ashbury area in the late 1960s, the Castro had become the epicentre of gay life in America. Maupin's columns were the basis for his subsequent bestselling *Tales of the City* series of novels, which featured characters from across the sexual spectrum – the central gay character was Michael 'Mouse' Tolliver, who seemed to be the alter ego of Maupin himself.

Anita Bryant was a singer, former beauty queen and born-again Christian. She had appeared in adverts for companies including Tupperware and Kraft Foods, and was the spokesperson for the Florida Citrus Commission. In 1977 she started a campaign to repeal recently granted gay rights in Miami under the banner 'Save Our Children' – it was depressingly successful.

Maupin, a US Navy veteran, had been raised in a conservative family in still-segregated North Carolina – he didn't come out until he was thirty and living on the West Coast. He wrote the fictional 'Letter to Mama' in the voice of Michael Tolliver at the height of Bryant's campaign and it was published in the *San Francisco Chronicle*, the newspaper in which his column now appeared. It would serve as an inspiration to a whole generation of LGBTQ people wishing to come out to their own parents and families.

Michael's Letter to Mama

Dear Mama,

I'm sorry it's taken me so long to write. Every time I try to write to you and Papa I realize I'm not saying the things that are in my heart. That would be O.K., if I loved you any less than I do, but you are still my parents and I am still your child.

I have friends who think I'm foolish to write this letter. I hope they're wrong. I hope their doubts are based on parents who loved and trusted them less than mine do. I hope especially that you'll see this as an act of love on my part, a sign of my continuing need to share my life with you. I wouldn't have written, I guess, if you hadn't told me about your involvement in the Save Our Children campaign. That, more than anything, made it clear that my responsibility was to tell you the truth, that your own child is homosexual, and that I never needed saving from anything except the cruel and ignorant piety of people like Anita Bryant.

I'm sorry, Mama. Not for what I am, but for how you must feel at this moment. I know what that feeling is, for I felt it for most of my life. Revulsion, shame, disbelief – rejection through fear of something I knew, even as a child, was as basic to my nature as the color of my eyes.

No, Mama, I wasn't "recruited." No seasoned homosexual ever served as my mentor. But you know what? I wish someone had. I wish someone older than me and wiser than the people in Orlando had taken me aside and said, "You're all right, kid. You can grow up to be a doctor or a teacher just like anyone else. You're not crazy or sick or evil. You can succeed and be happy and find peace with friends – all kinds of friends – who don't give a damn who you go to bed with. Most of all, though, you can love and be loved, without hating yourself for it."

But no one ever said that to me, Mama. I had to find it out on my own, with the help of the city that has become my home. I know this may be hard for you to believe, but San Francisco is full of men and women, both straight and gay, who don't consider sexuality in measuring the worth of another human being.

These aren't radicals or weirdos, Mama. They are shop clerks and bankers and little old ladies and people who nod and smile to you when you meet them on the bus. Their attitude is neither patronizing nor pitying. And their message is so simple: Yes, you are a person. Yes, I like you. Yes, it's all right for you to like me, too.

I know what you must be thinking now. You're asking yourself: What did we do wrong? How did we let this happen? Which one of us made him that way?

I can't answer that, Mama. In the long run, I guess I really don't care. All I know is this: If you and Papa are responsible for the way I am, then I thank you with all my heart, for it's the light and the joy of my life.

I know I can't tell you what it is to be gay. But I can tell you what it's not.

It's not hiding behind words, Mama. Like family and decency and Christianity. It's not fearing your body, or the pleasures that God made for it. It's not judging your neighbor, except when he's crass or unkind.

Being gay has taught me tolerance, compassion and humility. It has shown me the limitless possibilities of living. It has given me people whose passion and kindness and sensitivity have provided a constant source of strength. It has brought me into the family of man, Mama, and I like it here. I like it.

There's not much else I can say, except that I'm the same Michael you've always known. You just know me better now. I have never consciously done anything to hurt you. I never will.

Please don't feel you have to answer this right away. It's enough for me to know that I no longer have to lie to the people who taught me to value the truth.

Mary Ann sends her love.

Everything is fine at 28 Barbary Lane.

Your loving son,
Michael

47

Harvey Milk's Letter to Jimmy Carter on Gay Rights, 1978

Harvey Milk was the first openly gay man in the United States to win an election for public office. He had moved from working on Wall Street and voting for Nixon to living out and proud in the Castro district of San Francisco; after opening a camera shop there in 1972, he soon became involved in local politics, promoting gay, minority and union rights, and other liberal causes.

Milk won a seat on the San Francisco City-County Board in 1978 and used his platform to fight against California Proposition 6, an initiative proposed by the conservative Orange County state legislator John Briggs, that would have barred gays and lesbians, and possibly anyone who supported gay rights, from working in the state's schools. Milk's letter to Jimmy Carter secured the Democratic President's support in opposing the Briggs Initiative, which was eventually defeated by a substantial margin. Ronald Reagan, the Governor of California and Carter's successor in the White House, was also persuaded by Milk to oppose the bill.

After only eleven months in office, Milk, together with the city's Mayor, George Moscone, was assassinated in San Francisco City Hall by Dan White, a disgruntled former colleague.

Board of Supervisors,
City Hall, San Francisco 94102
Supervisor Harvey Milk

June 28, 1978

President Jimmy Carter
The White House
Washington, D.C. 20500

Dear President Carter:

There has been considerable press coverage of the speech I delivered at San Francisco's large Gay Freedom Day Celebrations this weekend.

In it, I called upon you to take a leadership role in defending the rights of gay people. As the President of a nation which includes 15–20 million lesbians and gay men, your leadership is vital and necessary. [. . .]

On the November, 1978, California ballot will be an initiative, called the Briggs Initiative, which would prohibit gay persons from teaching and would have other serious infringements on individual rights. Though it is a state ballot issue, it is also of great national importance and we hope you will strongly oppose it.

I would very much appreciate a response to our call for your support and I would be honored to work with you to protect the human rights of all Americans.

Warmly,
Harvey Milk

48
The Women of Greenham Common's Letter to Women on Nuclear War, 1981

In August 1981, thirty-six women, four men and several children walked 120 miles from Cardiff to RAF Greenham Common to protest against NATO's decision to site ninety-six American Tomahawk cruise nuclear missiles on the Berkshire air base – one that had been an expanse of open public land until the Second World War.

Affiliated with a Welsh feminist pacifist group called 'Women for Life on Earth' who were concerned about the Cold War and the growing threat of nuclear weapons, they arrived to deliver a letter to the base commander expressing their opposition to any escalation of the arms race. Unable to meet the commander in person, they set up an impromptu camp outside the gates. By September it had become a more permanent settlement and, significantly, a camp for women only, which remained open until 2000.

Rejecting hierarchical command structures, the protesters used chain letters and circulars to raise publicity and to encourage other women to participate in non-violent demonstrations at the base that were 'initiated rather than organised'. Letter-writing, along with more physical protests such as camp members chaining themselves to railings, was a serious component of the group's activities, as Alice Cook, one Greenham Common protester, later recalled:

> I had been to the camp several times but had not taken an active part for a few months. The letter came out of the blue . . . I didn't read so-called 'impartial' information in a newspaper. This was a personal communication addressed to me, requesting things of me, making it plain that every

woman was included, was important. Not only did I copy the letter, but I spent a long time considering who to send it to. I didn't send it to women who I thought would hear about the action anyway, nor to women who would never go to such a demonstration. I sent letters to women I thought would be interested but had not become directly involved. I felt that the spur of a personal letter might spark off enthusiasm.

Dear women,

The US air base at Greenham Common in Berkshire is the first place in Europe where 96 Cruise missiles are to be sited in December 1983. Since September 1981 women have been camping outside the main gate of the air base, protesting against this decision which has been taken without consulting the people of this country . . .

As women we have been actively encouraged to stay at home and look up to men as our protectors. But we reject this role. We cannot stand by while others are organizing to destroy life on our earth. It is not enough to go on demonstrations. We must find other ways of expressing the strengths of our opposition to this madness. We have one year left in which to reverse the Government's decision about Cruise missiles. There is still time to stop them.

With peace and love, from the women at Greenham Common

49

Deirdre Rhys-Thomas's Letter to Dr Benjamin Spock on Nuclear War, 1985

Deirdre Rhys-Thomas had been astounded when her twelve-year-old son Theo asked her if there was likely to be a nuclear war. Unable to respond convincingly either way, she embarked on a letter-writing spree to people in the public eye, in the hope of securing answers to calm her own fears and placate Theo's anxieties. Among the people she wrote to were the editor of the *Sun*, the head of British Petroleum and the scientists at IBM who were working on the 'Stars Wars' weapons programme.

First published in 1946, *The Common Sense Book of Baby and Child Care* by the American paediatrician Dr Benjamin Spock went on to become one of the bestselling books of the twentieth century. Credited by *Time* magazine with singlehandedly changing the way parents raised their children, in the late 1960s Spock became a leading activist in the anti-Vietnam war movement. Defending his apparently radical political stance, he maintained: 'It isn't enough to bring up children happy and secure, you need to provide a decent world for them. And this is why I have expanded my horizon.' In 1968 Spock was given a two-year jail sentence for aiding resistance to the draft, though he would never serve it.

10 July 1985

Dear Dr Spock,

I've not had the chance to read your new edition of *Baby and Child Care* but what really interests me is reading yesterday an article mentioning that you've got a chapter on the importance of parents becoming politically active to make a better World for their children and to preserve it from annihilation.

Four years ago my son Theo, then 12, asked me that question which all Mothers must dread hearing, 'Will there be nuclear war?'

You know I was totally unable to cope. I mean I was frightened for Theo and myself, it brought up all my own fears, my guilt that I'd let these politicians build up their nuclear weapons, and pure unleashed anger that my child should be burdened with this fear.

All I could rely on and by guided by was my maternal instincts, my intuition.

Theo's now 16 and only the other day he thanked me for visiting Greenham Common and Molesworth, and having written to the nuclear authorities questioning their attitudes.

And although he says the World is no safer indeed he feels it is more dangerous – he was quite happy seeing *Star Wars* on the cinema screen but he doesn't want it up above his head – he feels able to cope because he knows I will do all I can to protect him, and love him. In this my husband, Peter, has been so understanding and supportive.

But, Dr Spock, I don't know about getting politically active. The track record of successive British Governments on the nuclear issue had been appalling.

We've had a By-Election in our region. It created much media interest because it brought out 'the Thatcher factor' – a rejection of Mrs Thatcher's dictatorial ways – and yet I wonder how many of these voters were her ardent 'Argie-bashers' round the Falklands War?

What's worrying parents round here is not enough money for their children's school books, schools promised and not built, lollipop school crossing patrols stopped, yet few parents at meetings suggest that the £11 billion to be spent on Trident – a mere £500 million each year for the next 20 years so the Defence Minister has said – should be spent instead on those necessary requirements.

You know, Dr Spock, I have a dream. Women, Mothers in the World getting themselves together – never mind the political opinion – but for their children and becoming politically-wise, educating themselves about all things nuclear, and taking on those over-blown, over-opinionated negotiators at the Geneva Arms Talks. What's wrong with Mothers of the World sitting in on the talks? We have to answer our children's nuclear fears.

Yours sincerely,
Deirdre Rhys-Thomas

Benjamin Spock, M.D., Arkansas

Aug 5 1985

Dear Mrs Thomas,

Thanks for writing. I still believe that citizens can change the course of government if they will overcome their cynicism and inertia. (In America only half the citizens bother to vote.) Of course the answer to not enough money for schools is to stop wasting it on nuclear arms that only make us all more insecure.

My answer to children's questions about nuclear annihilation would be, 'It could happen but it doesn't have to if we would all vote, lobby.' The parent can tell what she or he is doing, and suggest that the child write a letter to the prime minister, or president, or MP or MC.

It was through political activity that slavery was ended, child labor was stopped and women got the vote.

Sincerely,
Ben Spock

50

Olusegun Obasanjo's Letter to Margaret Thatcher on Apartheid, 1986

Olusegun Obasanjo, the general, statesman and diplomat, served as Nigeria's military ruler between 1976 and 1979 before handing power over to a democratic government. He was also its civilian and elected president from 1999 to 2007. In 1986 he issued the following stinging critique of Margaret Thatcher, who had referred to the African National Congress as a 'terrorist' organisation and also opposed sanctions on South Africa, then under the rule of P.W. Botha, as a means to hasten the end of apartheid.

Downing Street papers released in 2016 revealed that in 1986, Thatcher's Foreign Secretary Sir Geoffrey Howe had called for the Prime Minster to condemn apartheid as 'totally repugnant'. In the absence of her making any such robust statement, Howe was dispatched on a state visit to South Africa in advance of that year's Commonwealth Games, where he was nevertheless snubbed by both Botha and members of the opposition ANC.

August 1986

Dear Margaret,

After our meeting on Sunday, I write as one committed democrat to another. Yours is an old country with a lengthy democratic tradition; mine a new country undergoing a press of nation-building. But as democrats, we can be frank with each other.

As you know, I came to the EPG (Eminent Persons' Group) mission with reluctance. It was difficult enough for me as an African and especially as a Nigerian to contemplate exchanging pleasantries with those responsible for the institutionalised oppression of so many of my brothers and sisters.

My repugnance was exacerbated by the widely held perception that the EPG was a substitute for action won by you at Nassau for the benefit of P.W. Botha. However, I persuaded myself that whatever the odds, the prize was so great that I should overcome my personal feelings.

Not that I was prepared for what we found. As you know, even Tony Barber – a frequent traveller to South Africa – was appalled by what he was to see in that other South Africa which visitors seldom see. We jointly expressed our shock and dismay in our report.

I have seen extremes of poverty and of oppression in many parts of the world. But South Africa unashamedly moulds both elements into a system which enables the white minority to enjoy a "Dallas" lifestyle at the expense of the great majority forced to endure conditions as degrading as anything I have seen anywhere.

In our discussions, Malcolm Fraser and I tried to convey the true nature of the system and were against cosmetic changes which have merely softened the face of apartheid.

However, such was our discussion that I must ask: Did you even read our report?

I infer from what you said that afternoon that you had not. You concentrated on the trivia of the Government's "reforms" – like the welcome but essentially insignificant repeal of the Mixed Marriages Act – and ignored their implacable opposition to changes in the basic pillars of apartheid.

As we emphasised, to begin to dismantle apartheid, the Population Registration Act and the Group Areas Act must be repealed without being replaced by some measure designed to achieve the same ends under a different guise.

You gave credence to the dangerous notion that the political rights of the dispossessed can be adequately met by what President Botha calls "group rights" at the expense of individual rights and freedoms. Despite all the talk of "power sharing" between different communities, our inescapable conclusion was that this was a cloak for power remaining in white hands, and the essentials of apartheid continuing unchanged.

Nor have you any appreciation of the issue of violence. The apartheid system has an inherent violence which, through forced removals and the creation of barren homelands, has created the fiction of a white land and through the barrel of the gun, denies blacks any form of legitimate political expression.

We are all opposed to violence other than in self-defence. Why should blacks not have a right to defend their own families, homes and freedoms?

Your "moral revulsion" for sanctions struck me as unconvincing. The economic sanctions you so energetically pursued against Poland, Afghanistan and Argentina were brushed aside in your determination to withhold their application to South Africa. Yet to many of us there is only one significant difference: the victims in South Africa are black. Is sauce for the Aryan goose not sauce for the Negroid gander?

Your concentration on the economic effectiveness of sanctions is disingenuous if not hypocritical. Sanctions were imposed against Poland, Afghanistan and Argentina as political expressions of outrage.

Nor can your opposition be based on any assessment of where the best interests of Britain lie. Your country has considerable trade with South Africa, but this is dwarfed by that enjoyed with the rest of Africa: it cannot be in Britain's interests to encourage them to place their orders elsewhere. Further, your appearance as an apologist challenges the democratic forces in South Africa to seek help from whatever quarter they can. The longer-term consequences for Britain, the United States and the West could be considerable.

But most of all, I was dismayed by your lack of vision. You offered no action as an alternative to sanctions. You insisted that nothing whatever be done – even though in the final analysis you moved a little. There is no vision of a way ahead; simply a forlorn hope that P.W. Botha would experience a "Road to Damascus" conversion on the road to Soweto. Such hopes are in vain. Sooner or later, Botha or his successor will be driven to negotiate meaningfully. Sir Geoffrey's visit again confirmed that Botha is not yet under sufficient pressure to do so – despite a dwindling rand, escalating inflation, a declining economy and mounting violence. More pressure must come.

I must tell you that many people around the world view your continued opposition to sanctions as founded on instinct, not logic and as displaying a misguided tribal loyalty and myopic political vision. The consequences of such perceptions are far-reaching for a country which has traditionally claimed the high ground of principle.

Not only does the mental laager of the Boer seem to be mirrored in your own attitudes, but his fatal concessions of too little, too late are paralleled by your actions.

I am glad that the Commonwealth has moved on without you and I know that sooner rather than later, Britain will have to join us. I also know that apartheid will end, and its demise will be the product of a combination of internal and external pressures. The equation is a simple one. The less the external pressure, the greater will be the price to be paid internally.

Those who seek to minimise sanctions and their effect will have the blood of thousands, if not millions, of innocents on their hands and on their consciences. My heart will be heavy but my hands will be clean. Will yours?

51

Alex Molnar's Letter to the *New York Times* on the Gulf War, 1990

Alex Molnar was in 1990 a professor of education at the University of Wisconsin in Milwaukee. His twenty-one-year-old son Chris, while serving in the US Marine Corps, was posted to Saudi Arabia in the First Gulf War in 1990.

Molnar did not consider himself an anti-war activist nor a peace campaigner, but he was fundamentally opposed to what he considered an 'unnecessary military offensive' in the Persian Gulf, one for which he believed 'a 'diplomatic solution' should have been found. Accordingly he wrote letter to President Bush, and sent it to the White House and the *New York Times*, who published it in August 1990.

While he received no response from the White House, among those who did write back to him was Judy Davenport, the wife of a career navy man, and the pair would together establish the Military Families Support Network. This was an anti-Gulf War group composed largely of people who had relatives stationed in the Persian Gulf, as well as veterans and members of military families. Their message was: 'Support the troops. Stop fighting. Start talking.'

If My Marine Son Is Killed . . . I Won't Forgive You, Mr President

August 29, 1990

Dear President Bush:

I kissed my son goodbye today.

He is a 21-year-old Marine.

You have ordered him to Saudi Arabia.

The letter telling us he was going arrived at our vacation cottage in northern Wisconsin by Express Mail on Aug. 13. We left immediately for North Carolina to be with him. Our vacation was over.

Some commentators say you are continuing your own vacation to avoid appearing trapped in the White House, as President Carter was during the Iran hostage crisis. Perhaps that is your reason.

However, as I sat in my motel room watching you on television, looking through my son's hastily written last will and testament and listening to military equipment rumble past, you seemed to me to be both callous and ridiculous chasing golf balls and zipping around in your boat in Kennebunkport.

While visiting my son, I had a chance to see him pack his chemical-weapons suit and try on his body armor. I don't know if you've ever had this experience, Mr. President. I hope you never will.

I also met many of my son's fellow soldiers. They are fine young men.

A number told me that they were from poor families.

They joined the Marines as a way of earning enough money to go to college.

None of the young men I met are likely to be invited to serve on the board of directors of a savings and loan association, as your son Neil was.

And none of them have parents well enough connected to call or write a general to ensure that their child stays out of harm's way, as Vice President Dan Quayle's parents did for him during the Vietnam War.

I read in the *Raleigh News and Observer* that, like you, Quayle and Secretary of State James Baker were on vacation. Meanwhile, Defense Secretary Dick Cheney was in the Persian Gulf.

I think this symbolizes a government that no longer has a non-military foreign-policy vision, one that uses the military to conceal the fraud that American diplomacy has become.

Yes, you have proved a relatively adept tactician in the last three weeks. But if American diplomacy hadn't been on vacation for the better part of a decade, we wouldn't be in the spot we are today.

Where were you, Mr. President, when Iraq was killing its own people with poison gas? Why, until the recent crisis, was it business as usual with Saddam Hussein, the man you now call a Hitler?

You were elected vice president in 1980 on the strength of the promise of a better life for Americans, in a world where the United States would once again "stand tall."

The Reagan-Bush administration rolled into Washington talking about the magic of a "free market" in oil. You diluted gas-mileage requirements for cars and dismantled federal energy policy.

And now you have ordered my son to the Middle East.

For what?

Cheap gasoline?

Is the American "way of life" that you say my son is risking his life for the continued "right" of Americans to consume 25 percent to 30 percent of the world's oil?

The "free market" to which you are so fervently devoted has a very high price tag, at least for parents like me and young men and women like my son.

Now that we face the prospect of war, I intend to support my son and his fellow soldiers by doing everything I can to oppose any offensive American military action in the Persian Gulf. The troops I met deserve far better than the politicians and policies that hold them hostage.

As my wife and I sat in a little cafe outside our son's base last week, trying to eat, fighting back tears, a young Marine struck up a conversation with us. As we parted he wished us well and said, "May God forgive us for what we are about to do."

President Bush, the policies you have advocated for the last decade have set the stage for military conflict in the Middle East. Your response to the Iraqi conquest of Kuwait has set in motion events that increasingly will pressure you to use our troops not to defend Saudi Arabia but to attack Iraq.

And I'm afraid that, as that pressure mounts, you will wager my son's life in a gamble to save your political future.

In the past, you have demonstrated no enduring commitment to any principle other than the advancement of your political career.

This makes me doubt that you have either the courage or the character to meet the challenge of finding a diplomatic solution to this crisis.

If, as I expect, you eventually order American soldiers to attack Iraq, then it is God who will have to forgive you. I will not.

Alex Molnar

52

Phyllis and Orlando Rodriguez's Letter to the *New York Times* on Terrorism, 2001

On 11 September 2001, Islamic extremists connected to the al-Qaeda terrorist group, founded and led by the Saudi-born Osama bin Laden, hijacked four aeroplanes on the east coast of America. They flew two of them directly into the twin towers of the World Trade Center in New York, and a third into the Pentagon in Washington. The fourth, thanks to the crew and passengers overpowering its hijackers, never reached its intended target and crashed in a field in Pennsylvania. Close to 3,000 people, including the nineteen hijackers, lost their lives, in the worst terrorist atrocity that had ever occurred on American soil.

Amid cries for immediate and violent reprisals, Phyllis and Orlando Rodriguez, whose son was killed in the attack on the twin towers, wrote to the *New York Times*, urging caution.

15 September 2001

Our son Greg is among the many missing from the World Trade Center attack. Since we first heard the news, we have shared moments of grief, comfort, hope, despair, fond memories with his wife, the two families, our friends and neighbors, his loving colleagues at Cantor Fitzgerald / Espeed, and all the grieving families that daily meet at the Pierre Hotel. We see our hurt and anger reflected among everybody we meet. We cannot pay attention to the daily flow of news about this disaster. But we read enough of the news to sense that our government is heading in the direction of violent revenge, with the prospect of sons, daughters, parents, friends in distant lands dying, suffering, and nursing further grievances against us. It is not the way to go. It will not avenge our son's death. Not in our son's name. Our son died a victim of an inhuman ideology. Our actions should not serve the same purpose. Let us grieve. Let us reflect and pray. Let us think about a rational response that brings real peace and justice to our world. But let us not as a nation add to the inhumanity of our times.

Phyllis and Orlando Rodriguez

53

Tilda Swinton's Letter to the Late Derek Jarman on Art, 2002

Painter, filmmaker, gay rights campaigner and gardener, Derek Jarman's extraordinary body of work ranged from solo exhibitions at London's prestigious Lisson Gallery and producing sets for Ken Russell and the Royal Opera House, to making pop videos with the Smiths and the Pet Shop Boys. His films included *Sebastiane* (1976), a retelling of the story of the Christian martyr, whose nudity and homoerotic imagery caused controversy when it was first broadcast on television, and *The Tempest* (1979), a free-wheeling adaptation of Shakespeare's late play, starring the punk-pop singer Toyah Willcox. Willcox also appeared in *Jubilee* (1978), the film whose DVD release prompted Tilda Swinton, one of Jarman's long-standing collaborators, to write a letter in tribute to her late friend and mentor, which was published in the *Guardian*. Jarman had died in 1994 from AIDS-related bronchopneumonia, having tested positive for HIV in 1986 – the same year in which his much-delayed film *Caravaggio*, a fictional portrait of the Baroque painter and the first of his films to feature Swinton, was released.

Letter to an angel

17 July 2002

Dear Derek,

Jubilee is out on DVD. I found a copy in Inverness and watched it last night. It's as cheeky a bit of inspired old-ham, punk-spunk nonsense as ever grew out of your brain, and that's saying something; what a buzz it gives me to look at it now. And what a joke: there's nothing one-eighth as mad, bad and downright spiritualised being made down here these days this side of Beat Takeshi.

There's an interview with you at the end of the thing: a face-to-face. Very nice to see that face, I must say. Jeremy Isaacs asks you, last of all, how you would like to be remembered, and you say you would like to disappear. That you would like to take all your works with you and . . . evaporate.

It's a funny thing, because the truth is that, here, eight years later, in so many ways, you never could disappear, but – it has to be faced – in so many others you have. It has snowed since you were here and your tracks are covered. Fortunately, you made them on hard ground.

Well, I could tell you that we got some things right back then, sitting round the kitchen table in Dungeness, projectile-vomiting with the best of them: you were indeed the great Thatcherite film-maker – for every £200,000 film you made, real profits were seen (by someone or other) within at least the first two years; and all those royal circus brides did end up cutting themselves out of their wedding dresses and looking into the camera. Alan "all film is an advertisment for something" Parker did end up running the BFI and dissolving its production arm; and FilmFour was just a flash in the pan.

They talk about the British film industry a lot these days. You remember that renaissance they all got moist about in the 1980s after *Chariots of Fire* won four Oscars – "The British are coming"? And then that thing with *Henry V*? Well, the renaissances are rolling themselves out pretty much yearly now, as director after director makes his or her first film and then graduates to making commercials.

It felt as if industrial films on these islands in those 1980s were made by people who could not quite get into television. Or by shameless, traitorous expatriates who had legged it for the "free world". In those days, British Film Inc, when invoked, meant getting proud about *The Lavender Hill Mob* or *Whisky Galore!* An American-Indian partnership began to give Britain an exportable identity: these were the Crabtree and Evelyn Waugh days of post-imperial mooning about, when nostalgic dreams of the Grand Tour meant film culture to a lot of people. Class obsession – still the greatest stock in trade of industrial cinema here – began to show a profit.

I had run away to join a different circus myself: Planet Jarmania. You were the first person I met who could gossip about St

Thomas Aquinas and hold a steady camera at the same time. I thought it would be good to hang out with you for six weeks: I guess we had things to say. Our outfit was an internationalist brigade. Decidedly pre-industrial. A little loud, a lot louche. Not always in the best possible taste. And not quite fit, though it saddened and maddened us to recognise it, for wholesome family entertainment.

Wholesome families were all the rage then. There was a fashion for a thing called "normal" and there was a plague abroad called "perversion". There was no such thing as society, and culture meant something to do with yogurt (this was before the *Sunday Times* educated us that culture means digested opinions about marketable artistic endeavours). Things are different now: people (at least pretend to) have an enormous amount of sex and tell everybody else about it. We use the word terrestrial without a flicker of spacethink. People cook and decorate their flats and celebrate the millennium and the opening of the Commonwealth Games in cajun/Echo Park hacienda/ Alternative Miss World circa 1978 styles. Straight has started to mean honest again, getting very drunk is hilariously funny and smart, and newsreaders would refer to today as July seventeenth.

We used to be referred to as the arthouse; how it used to irk us then. How disparaging it sounded; how sickly and highfalutin; how pious and extracurricular. For arthouse superstar, read jumbo shrimp. Yet, then, as now, the myth prevailed that there was only one mainstream. We were only too happy to know that our audience existed and to hoe the row in peace. Nobody here paid that much attention to us, that's true: no one ever thought we might make them any money, I suppose.

What grace that constituted. Not to be identified as national product. The intergalactic BFI. ZDF in Germany. Mikado in Italy. Uplink in Japan. This was our nation state: this was continuity. We sneaked under the fence, looked for – and found – our fellow travellers elsewhere. Here's the thought: slice the world longways, along its lines of sensibility, and not straight up and down, through its geographical markers, and company will be yours, young film-maker. Treason? To what?

The dead hand of good taste has commenced its last great attempt to buy up every soul on the planet, and from where I'm sitting, it's going great guns. Art is now indivisible from the idea of culture, culture from heritage, heritage from tourism, tourism from what I saw emblazoned recently on the window of an American chain store in Glasgow – "the art of leisure". That means, incidentally, velours lounging suits by the ton.

The colonial balance has shifted and the long spoons are out. We now stand shoulder to shoulder with something identifiable as civilisation itself, or else . . . Security never felt so much like a term of abuse. I was in Los Angeles earlier this year and was asked by a jeweller's assistant in an emporium on Rodeo Drive if the reason I declined to wear a stars and stripes jewelled badge on my front at a public event was that I was "an Afghani bitch". You may not need me to tell you about the fight for civilisation afoot these days. More of the same, but worse than even you could have imagined. Meanwhile, in a binary world, we on these islands cream on creamily up a Third Way.

Things have got awfully tidy recently. There is a lot of finish on things. Clingfilm gloss and the neatest of hospital corners. The formula merchants are out in force. They are in the market for guaranteed product. They go out looking for film-makers with the nous of one who might consider employing halogen spotlights in the hopes of attracting wild cats into a suburban garden. They are missing the point. Don't they know the roulette wheel is fixed? That the croupier is a cardsharp? Do these people not watch old movies? It's the spirited that hold the hands in the long run, it always was – the low-key for the long term, the irreverent, the cheats, the undaunted and inspired rule-breakers, not the goody-goody industrial types with their bedside manners and managerial know-how.

It is all done with smoke and mirrors, and it always will be. Not with memos and steering groups. Not with statistical evidence or test screenings. Don't they know the basic laws of being in an audience? That we say we want to know more about the villain, but we don't really; that we say we like happy endings, but our souls droop without the bittersweet touch of something we might recognise, as we bend from our fascinating and complex mortal world into the virtual dark and back again. That we say we want famous faces we can recognise, but there's one thing that a face that we identify as an actor's first and foremost cannot do for us that the face we might see as that of a person can do. It is human beings that are of use to us in the figurative cinema. Human shapes and gauchenesses and human passions. Not drama and perfect timing and a well-tuned charisma round every bend.

I have always wholeheartedly treasured in your work the whiff of the school play. It tickles me still and I miss it terribly. The antidote it offers to the mirror ball of the marketable – the artful without the art, the meaningful devoid of meaning – is meat and drink to so many of us looking for that dodgy wig, that moment of awkward zing, that loose corner where we might prise up the carpet and uncover the rich slates of something we might recognise as spirit underneath. Something raw and dusty and inarticulate, for heaven's sake. This is what Pasolini knew. What Rossellini knew. This is also what Ken Loach knows. What Andrew Kotting knows. What Powell and Pressburger, what William Blake knew. And, for that matter, what Caravaggio knew, painting prostitutes as Madonnas and rent boys as saints. No, Madonnas as prostitutes and saints as rent boys – there's the rub.

I think that the reason that you count for so much, so uniquely, to some people, particularly in this hidebound little place we call home, is that you lived so clearly the life that an artist lives. Your money was always where your mouth was. Your vocation – and here maybe it helped a little that you offered that special combination of utter self-obsession with the appearance of the kindest Jesuit classics master in the school – was a spiritual one, even more than it was political, even more than it was artistic. And the clarity with which you offered up your life and the living of it, particularly since the epiphany – I can call it nothing less – of your illness was a genius stroke, not only of provocation, but of grace.

Your gesture of public confessional, both within and without your work – at a time when people talked fairly openly about setting up ostracised HIV island communities and others feared not only for their lives but, believe it or not, for their jobs, their insurance policies, their friendships, their civil rights – was made with such particular, and characteristically inclusive, generosity that it was at that point that you made an impact far outspanning the influence of your work. You made your spirit known to us – and

Together we are stronger than the fear and ignorance attempting to tear us and our families apart. We cannot accept silent inaction. We cannot rest until we have justice for your daughters and for all girls and boys kept out of school.

Ziauddin Yousafzai

the possibility of an artist's fearlessness a reality. And the truth of it is, by defying it, you may have changed the market as well.

That earlier Jubilee year you gave us prophecy – painting extinct in Paranoia Paradise, the generation who grew up and forgot to lead their lives, the idea of artists as the world's blood donors, history written on a Mandrax, fear of dandelions – and yet, like Carnation from Floris, not all the good things have disappeared.

Maybe now it is as bad as you and I used to say it could possibly get. Maybe it's worse. But here we are, the rest of us, tilting at the same old, same old windmills and spooking at the same old ghosts. And keeping company, all the same. It's a rotten mess of a shambles, you could say. It's driving into the curve, at the very least. Some would say you are well out of it. I reckon you would say: "Let me at 'em."

The challenges facing a film culture today? The possibility of film-makers losing the use of their own spirits. The paralysis of isolated, original voices. The existence of the student loan in the place of the student grant. The rarity of distributors with kamikaze vision. Too many conference tables. Too few cinemas. Too little patience. Pomp and circumstance. The concept of the "successful" product. The idea that there is not enough to go around. The eye to the main chance. The substitution of codependence for independence. The idea that it has to cost millions of pounds to make a feature film. The idea that there is only one way to skin a cat.

This is what I miss, now that there are no more Derek Jarman films: the mess, the cant, the poetry, Simon Fisher Turner's music, the real faces, the intellectualism, the bad-temperedness, the good-temperedness, the cheek, the standards, the anarchy, the romanticism, the classicism, the optimism, the activism, the glee, the bumptiousness, the resistance, the wit, the fight, the colours, the grace, the passion, the beauty.

Longlivemess.
Longlivepassion.
Longlivecompany.

yr,
Tild

54

Alice Walker's Open Letter to Barack Obama on his Election, 2008

On 4 November 2008, Illinois Senator Barack Obama was elected President of the United States. The forty-fourth incumbent, he was also the first African-American to achieve this office. Having been elected into the House of Representatives only four years earlier, he had seen off the far more experienced and well-known candidate, Senator Hillary Rodham Clinton, for the Democratic presidential nomination. Against considerable odds, but buoyed by strong support from younger voters enthused and energised by his optimistic 'Yes We Can' slogan and the innovative use of digital campaigning, he convincingly defeated his Republican opponent, the seasoned Arizona Senator and Vietnam veteran John S. McCain.

Alice Walker was raised in Georgia in the segregated South during the 'Jim Crow' era, the child of sharecroppers. A novelist, essayist, poet and civil rights campaigner, she was the first African-American woman to win the Pulitzer Prize for Fiction in 1983 with her novel *The Color Purple*, which was later adapted into an award-winning film by Steven Spielberg. In an open letter, written the day after Obama's victory was announced and published in the *Root*, an online magazine that focuses on African-American culture, Walker reflected on the historic prospect of a black man occupying the White House for the first time.

---

5 November 2008

Dear Brother Obama,

You have no idea, really, of how profound this moment is for us. Us being the black people of the Southern United States. You think you know, because you are thoughtful, and you have studied our history. But seeing you deliver the torch so many others before you carried, year after year, decade after decade, century after century, only to be struck down before igniting the flame of justice and of law, is almost more than the heart can bear. And yet, this observation is not intended to burden you, for you are of a different time, and, indeed, because of all the relay runners before you, North America is a different place. It is really only to say: Well done. We knew, through all the generations, that you were with us, in us, the best of the spirit of Africa and of the Americas. Knowing this, that you would actually appear, someday, was part of our strength. Seeing you take your rightful place, based solely on your wisdom, stamina and character, is a balm for the weary warriors of hope, previously only sung about.

I would advise you to remember that you did not create the disaster that the world is experiencing, and you alone are not responsible for bringing the world back to balance. A primary responsibility that you do have, however, is to cultivate happiness in your own life. To make a schedule that permits sufficient time of rest and play with your gorgeous wife and lovely daughters. And so on. One gathers that your family is large. We are used to seeing men in the White House soon become juiceless and as white-haired as the building; we notice their wives and children looking strained and stressed. They soon have smiles so lacking in joy that they remind us of scissors. This is no way to lead. Nor does your family deserve this fate. One way of thinking about all this is: It is so bad now that there is no excuse not to relax. From your happy, relaxed state, you can model real success, which is all that so many people in the world really want. They may buy endless cars and houses and furs and gobble up all the attention and space they can manage, or barely manage, but this is because it is not yet clear to them that success is truly an inside job. That it is within the reach of almost everyone.

I would further advise you not to take on other people's enemies. Most damage that others do to us is out of fear, humiliation and pain. Those feelings occur in all of us, not just in those of us who profess a certain religious or racial devotion. We must learn actually not to have enemies, but only confused adversaries who are ourselves in disguise. It is understood by all that you are commander in chief of the United States and are sworn to protect our beloved country; this we understand, completely. However, as my mother used to say, quoting a Bible with which I often fought, "hate the sin, but love the sinner." There must be no more crushing of whole communities, no more torture, no more dehumanizing as a means of ruling a people's spirit. This has already happened to people of color, poor people, women, children. We see where this leads, where it has led.

A good model of how to "work with the enemy" internally is presented by the Dalai Lama, in his endless caretaking of his soul as he confronts the Chinese government that invaded Tibet. Because, finally, it is the soul that must be preserved, if one is to remain a credible leader. All else might be lost; but when the soul dies, the connection to earth, to peoples, to animals, to rivers, to mountain ranges, purple and majestic, also dies. And your smile, with which we watch you do gracious battle with unjust characterizations, distortions and lies, is that expression of healthy self-worth, spirit and soul, that, kept happy and free and relaxed, can find an answering smile in all of us, lighting our way, and brightening the world.

We are the ones we have been waiting for.

In Peace and Joy,
Alice Walker

55

Tony Benn's Letter to his Grandchildren on Changing the World, 2009

The politician, writer, diarist and former BBC radio producer Anthony Wedgwood Benn (nicknamed 'Wedgie the Whizz' during his spell as the Minister of Technology in Harold Wilson's 1960s Labour government) came from a political family. His father and both his grandfathers had been members of parliament, as, in due course, was his second son, Hilary. The product of an elite background, Benn once ruefully observed that his contribution to the Labour Party was that he knew 'the British establishment inside out' and what they were 'up to'. Benn joined the Labour Party as a teenager in 1942 and retired from the House of Commons in 2001, some fifty-one years after first becoming an MP. A teetotal, tea-drinking pipe-smoker, he confessed to growing more left-wing as he grew older. In later years he was a familiar presence on television and radio discussion programmes, and a leading figure in the Stop the War Coalition, a group formed in September 2001 to protest against military action in Iraq and Afghanistan and George Bush's so-called 'war on terror' following the 9/11 attacks.

In 2009, at the age of eighty-four, Benn and his editor Ruth Winstone produced a book of letters, in which the politician attempted to offer his grandchildren some advice for the future.

In the first letter Benn stated:

> Every generation has to fight the same battles for peace, justice and democracy, and there is no *final* victory nor *final* defeat. Your generation will have to take up its own battles.

These are the ideas which led me to write this book, and I address them to you but also to your generation in the hope that they give you all encouragement to develop ways of safeguarding mankind and making life better for humanity.

Dear Nahal, Michael, James, William, Jonathan, Caroline, Emily, Daniel, Hannah and Sarah[. . .]

You must often ask yourselves whether it is possible to change the world in which you live. Given a population of nearly 7 billion people, it is understandable that you might feel impotent to change anything by your individual effort. But by accepting the world as it is you legitimise it and thereby become responsible in part for its iniquities.

There are four questions which, although simple, and even child-like, get to the heart of the problem and offer a way for adults to act.

Where there is injustice, the first question is: who gave one person the right to do harm to another?

That is a revolutionary question which is directed at authority itself and the sources of power which sustain it.

Then comes the question: what is going on? It is often a difficult one to answer but it is also an important one because if you do not understand a situation you cannot influence it.

The next question is: why is it going on? It forces you to think about the nature of society and how it works.

What can you do about it? is the most difficult but also the most important question of all.

History gives you examples of people who have challenged injustice.

First, there are the teachers who have attempted to explain the world: Moses, Jesus, Mohammed, Buddha and the founders of the world's religions, who have all tried to layout some moral principles which should guide us in our lives. In this category you will also find Galileo, Darwin, Marx, Gandhi, Einstein, Tutu and all those whose influence has been felt long after the kings, emperors and presidents were forgotten.

What they said has been tested and proved to be influential.

The next group of people who have left deep footprints in the sands of time are those who have combined into movements and campaigned – sometimes successfully, sometimes not – but at least they have tried. You can learn from their failures just as much as from their successes.

If you approach your life with these questions and ideas in mind, you gain confidence, and self-confidence is an immensely important factor: the rich and powerful have confidence in themselves because they have at their disposal the means to do what they want.

The least confident are those who have no wealth or power and see themselves as the permanent victims of injustice, actually persuading themselves that there is nothing that can be done to change those injustices.

In this sense confidence is a class issue, because the wealthy and powerful convey their confidence to their own children, and nowhere is this more apparent than in the private education system. That is why the comprehensive system is so important – it instills confidence in the working-class children who form the majority of pupils.

What has always frightened the rich and powerful has been the appearance from among the oppressed of self-confident leaders who prove their strength by organising in a way that could alter the balance of power.

In the days of empire such people were dismissed as 'uppity natives', just as working-class leaders in the trade union movement have been condemned for questioning the existing power structure.

This is why encouragement is the most important thing that can be given; a teacher at school who offers encouragement gives his pupils the faith to carry on, and the old should encourage the young rather than complain and put them down.

56

Stephen Fry's Open Letter to David Cameron and the International Olympic Committee on Homophobia, 2013

In June 2013, Russian President Putin signed into law a bill that banned what was termed 'propaganda of non-traditional sexual relations'. In effect, these new rules introduced the official stigmatisation of LGBTQ relationships in Russia, making it a criminal offence to equate them with heterosexual relationships. Gay pride rallies and the sharing or publication of information about lesbian, gay, bisexual and transgender lifestyles were outlawed at a stroke and punishable with hefty fines.

That such prejudiced and punitive legislation had been passed just a year before Russia was to host the Winter Olympics outraged the actor and activist Stephen Fry, who wrote to the British Prime Minister David Cameron and the International Olympic Committee (IOC) calling for the country to stripped of the games.

7 August 2013

Dear Prime Minister, M. Rogge, Lord Coe and Members of the International Olympic Committee,

I write in the earnest hope that all those with a love of sport and the Olympic spirit will consider the stain on the Five Rings that occurred when the 1936 Berlin Olympics proceeded under the exultant aegis of a tyrant who had passed into law, two years earlier, an act which singled out for special persecution a minority whose only crime was the accident of their birth. In his case he banned Jews from academic tenure or public office, he made sure that the police turned a blind eye to any beatings, thefts or humiliations inflicted on them, he burned and banned books written by them.

He claimed they "polluted" the purity and tradition of what it was to be German, that they were a threat to the state, to the children and the future of the Reich. He blamed them simultaneously for the mutually exclusive crimes of Communism and for the controlling of international capital and banks. He blamed them for ruining the culture with their liberalism and difference. The Olympic movement at that time paid precisely no attention to this evil and proceeded with the notorious Berlin Olympiad, which provided a stage for a gleeful Führer and only increased his status at home and abroad. It gave him confidence. All historians are agreed on that. What he did with that confidence we all know.

Putin is eerily repeating this insane crime, only this time against LGBT Russians. Beatings, murders and humiliations are ignored by the police. Any defence or sane discussion of homosexuality is against the law. Any statement, for example, that Tchaikovsky was gay and that his art and life reflects this sexuality and are an inspiration to other gay artists would be punishable by imprisonment. It is simply not enough to say that gay Olympians may or may not be safe in their village. The IOC absolutely must take a firm stance on behalf of the shared humanity it is supposed to represent against the barbaric, fascist law that Putin has pushed through the Duma. Let us not forget that Olympic events used not only to be athletic, they used to include cultural competitions. Let us realise that in fact, sport is cultural. It does not exist in a bubble outside society or politics. The idea that sport and politics don't connect is worse than disingenuous, worse than stupid. It is wickedly, wilfully wrong. Everyone knows politics interconnects with everything for "politics" is simply the Greek for "to do with the people".

An absolute ban on the Russian Winter Olympics of 2014 in Sochi is simply essential. Stage them elsewhere in Utah, Lillehammer, anywhere you like. At all costs Putin cannot be seen to have the approval of the civilised world.

He is making scapegoats of gay people, just as Hitler did Jews. He cannot be allowed to get away with it. I know whereof I speak. I have visited Russia, stood up to the political deputy who introduced the first of these laws, in his city of St Petersburg. I looked into the face of the man and, on camera, tried to reason with him, counter him, make him understand what he was doing. All I saw reflected back at me was what Hannah Arendt called, so memorably, "the banality of evil." A stupid man, but like so many tyrants, one with an instinct of how to exploit a disaffected people by finding scapegoats. Putin may not be quite as oafish and stupid as Deputy Milonov but his instincts are the same. He may claim that the "values" of Russia are not the "values" of the West, but this is absolutely in opposition to Peter the Great's philosophy, and against the hopes of millions of Russians, those not in the grip of that toxic mix of shaven headed thuggery and bigoted religion, those who are agonised by the rolling back of democracy and the formation of a new autocracy in the motherland that has suffered so much (and whose music, literature and drama, incidentally I love so passionately).

I am gay. I am a Jew. My mother lost over a dozen of her family to Hitler's anti-Semitism. Every time in Russia (and it is constantly) a gay teenager is forced into suicide, a lesbian "correctively" raped, gay men and women beaten to death by neo-Nazi thugs while the Russian police stand idly by, the world is diminished and I for one, weep anew at seeing history repeat itself.

"All that is needed for evil to triumph is for good men to do nothing," so wrote Edmund Burke. Are you, the men and women of the IOC going to be those "good" who allow evil to triumph?

The Summer Olympics of 2012 were one of the most glorious moments of my life and the life of my country. For there to be a Russian Winter Olympics would stain the movement forever and wipe away any of that glory. The Five Rings would finally be forever smeared, besmirched and ruined in the eyes of the civilised world.

I am begging you to resist the pressures of pragmatism, of money, of the oily cowardice of diplomats and to stand up resolutely and proudly for humanity the world over, as your movement is *pledged* to do. Wave your Olympic flag with pride as we gay men and women wave our Rainbow flag with pride. Be brave enough to live up to the oaths and protocols of your movement, which I remind you of verbatim below.

Rule 4: Cooperate with the competent public or private organisations and authorities in the endeavour to place sport at the service of humanity and thereby to promote peace.

Rule 6: Act against any form of discrimination affecting the Olympic Movement.

Rule 15: Encourage and support initiatives blending sport with culture and education.

I especially appeal to you, Prime Minister, a man for whom I have the utmost respect. As the leader of a party I have for almost all of my life opposed and instinctively disliked, you showed a determined, passionate and clearly honest commitment to LGBT rights and helped push gay marriage through both houses of our parliament in the teeth of vehement opposition from so many of your own side. For that I will always admire you, whatever other differences may lie between us. In the end I believe you know when a thing is wrong or right. Please act on that instinct now.

Yours in desperate hope for humanity
Stephen Fry

57
Edward Snowden's Open Letter on Mass Surveillance, 2013

A former member of the US Army Reserve who was discharged after breaking both his legs in a training exercise, Edward Snowden initially worked as a security guard at the National Security Agency (NSA) before his wizardry with computers earned him a post in IT at the Central Intelligence Agency (CIA). After leaving the CIA in 2009, he began doing various contract data and programming jobs and was in 2012 assigned to the NSA's unit in Hawaii. While there, Snowden began to harvest documents as evidence of the extent of covert surveillance he'd discovered was being routinely undertaken by the NSA on ordinary American citizens. Affronted by what he believed was an assault on individual liberties, he leaked some of the documents, examples of which were subsequently published in the *Guardian*, the *Washington Post* and *Der Spiegel*.

After fleeing to Hong Kong, Snowden took refuge in Russia to avoid extradition to America, where he faces charges of violating the Espionage Act – at the time of writing, he is still living in Moscow. His whistleblowing brought the tension between national security and personal privacy to the public's attention in a way that continues to cause debate.

To whom it may concern,

I have been invited to write to you regarding your investigation of mass surveillance.

I am Edward Joseph Snowden, formerly employed through contracts or direct hire as a technical expert for the United States National Security Agency, Central Intelligence Agency, and Defense Intelligence Agency.

In the course of my service to these organizations, I believe I witnessed systemic violations of law by my government that created a moral duty to act. As a result of reporting these concerns, I have faced a severe and sustained campaign of persecution that forced me from my family and home. I am currently living in exile under a grant of temporary asylum in the Russian Federation in accordance with international law.

I am heartened by the response to my act of political expression, in both the United States and beyond. Citizens around the world as well as high officials – including in the United States – have judged the revelation of an unaccountable system of pervasive surveillance to be a public service. These spying revelations have resulted in the proposal of many new laws and policies to address formerly concealed abuses of the public trust. The benefits to society of this growing knowledge are becoming increasingly clear at the same time as claimed risks are being shown to have been mitigated.

Though the outcome of my efforts has been demonstrably positive, my government continues to treat dissent as defection, and seeks to criminalize political speech with felony charges that provide no defense. However, speaking the truth is not a crime. I am confident that with the support of the international community, the government of the United States will abandon this harmful behavior. I hope that when the difficulties of this humanitarian situation have been resolved, I will be able to cooperate in the responsible finding of fact regarding reports in the media, particularly in regard to the truth and authenticity of documents, as appropriate and in accordance with the law.

I look forward to speaking with you in your country when the situation is resolved, and thank you for your efforts in upholding the international laws that protect us all.

With my best regards,
Edward Snowden
31 October 2013

58

Benedict Cumberbatch et al.'s Open Letter to David Cameron Calling for the Pardon of Gay and Bisexual Men, 2015

An apology for the persecution of the mathematician, Second World War codebreaker and pioneer of theoretical computer science and artificial intelligence, Alan Turing, was slow in coming. Turing was prosecuted for 'acts of gross indecency' in 1952, for his sexual relationship with another man. Forced to accept chemical castration in lieu of a prison sentence and ostracised professionally, he committed suicide two years later, aged forty-one. Prime Minister Gordon Brown finally issued an apology in 2009, while in 2012 Lord Sharkey called in the House of Lords for a full pardon, on the 100th anniversary of Turing's birth; this would not be granted until December 2013.

Yet Turing's was not an isolated case: until the passing of the Sexual Offences Act in 1967 decriminalised 'private' homosexual acts between men, thousands of others were treated just as inhumanely. The following open letter, signed by actors and activists, called on the government to pardon them as well.

31 January 2015

To Her Majesty's Government

Alan Turing was one of the greatest heroes of the twentieth century, a man whose work on the machines that deciphered the Enigma codes helped win World War II and who was pivotal in the development of modern computers. Winston Churchill said

Alan Turing "made the single biggest contribution to the Allied victory in World War II".

In 1952 Turing was prosecuted and convicted of gross indecency under Section 11 of the Criminal Law Amendment Act 1885. He chose chemical castration instead of a prison sentence. On 7th June 1954 he committed suicide. His story was recently depicted in the film *The Imitation Game.*

In 2009, an "unequivocal apology" for his appalling treatment was issued by then Prime Minister Gordon Brown. Following the apology and after receiving a request from the justice secretary Chris Grayling, Queen Elizabeth II granted Alan Turing a posthumous pardon under the Royal Prerogative of Mercy in 2013.

But Alan Turing was not alone.

The apology and pardon of Alan Turing are to be welcomed but ignores over 49,000 men who were convicted under the same law, many of whom took their own lives. An estimated 15,000 men are believed to still be alive.

The UK's homophobic laws made the lives of generations of gay and bisexual men intolerable. It is up to young leaders of today including The Duke and Duchess of Cambridge to acknowledge this mark on our history and not allow it to stand.

We call upon Her Majesty's government to begin a discussion about the possibility of a pardoning all the men, alive or deceased, who like Alan Turing, were convicted under the UK's "gross indecency" law (Section 11 of the Criminal Law Amendment Act 1885) and under other discriminatory anti-gay legislation.

Yours Sincerely,
Stephen Fry
Benedict Cumberbatch
Peter Tatchell
Morten Tyldum (Director of *The Imitation Game*)
Matthew Todd (Editor of *Attitude* Magazine)
Rachel Barnes (niece of Alan Turing)

59

Ziauddin Yousafzai's Letter to the Parents of the Abducted Chibok Girls on Female Education, 2015

On the night of 14 April 2014, members of Boko Haram, a militant Islamic group waging a long insurgency to create a caliphate in Northern Nigeria and vehemently opposed to the education of women, kidnapped 276 girls from the dormitory at the Government Girls' Secondary School in the town of Chibok. Though many of the girls have since escaped and others were freed following ransoms paid or deals brokered by the Nigerian government and the Red Cross, at the time of writing, over a hundred are still missing.

Ziauddin Yousafzai was running a co-educational school in Pakistan's Swat Valley region when Taliban militants swept through the area in 2007 and began enforcing a ban on girls' education. His own daughter Malala, whose education he'd encouraged and who kept a blog of her life under Taliban rule, was shot in the head by Taliban militants while travelling by bus to school on 9 October 2012. She survived, and in 2014 became the youngest person ever to win the Nobel Peace Prize for her 'struggle against the suppression of children and young people and for the right of all children to education'.

Ziauddin and Malala subsequently met with the families of the lost Chibok girls. In this letter Ziauddin offers them a further message of support and also stresses the vital importance of female education, no matter who attempts to restrict it.

7 February 2015

Dear parents of the kidnapped schoolgirls of Chibok,

My heart is heavy as I write to you on the eve of the 300th day since your beloved daughters have been taken from you. You are in my prayers every day. You have known a pain no parent should ever know.

It was this past July when Malala and I sat with you as you shared stories of your brave daughters, shed tears with you, and prayed with you for their safe return. We challenged President Goodluck Jonathan to meet with you, acknowledge your pain, acknowledge the sacrifice your daughters made to achieve an education, and promise his support.

Seven months later, I say not enough has been done. The world may turn their attention away, but my daughter Malala and I will not forget you nor your children. Like Malala, your children were targeted simply for being girls who love to learn.

Today, Malala and I call on President Goodluck Jonathan to take resolute action and increase the Nigerian government's efforts to bring your daughters home safe and alive. It is his duty and responsibility to ensure the welfare of all Nigerian citizens.

It is up to all of Nigeria and the global community to raise their voices louder and demand your girls be brought home safely.

Education is a pathway to opportunity but every day women and girls face unspeakable challenges in their journeys to a better life. This is why through the Malala Fund, our family has continued to give its funding to support teenage girls in Northern Nigeria to allow them to pursue their education despite the many challenges they face.

When Malala was attacked by extremists for her commitment to education, I struggled to understand such a devastating act of violence. Sadly, these threats are an everyday reality for millions of girls and boys around the world, with the recent attack on a school in my nation of Pakistan being yet another tragic reminder of the risks faced by students and teachers. A school is a sacred place, an institution of growth and learning where no child should ever fear violence or retribution. It is my wish to see your daughters return home and to their classrooms in order to continue with their education, in a safe and protected environment.

Together we are stronger than the fear and ignorance attempting to tear us and our families apart. We cannot accept silent inaction. We cannot rest until we have justice for your daughters and for all girls and boys kept out of school.

Malala and I continue to stand with you and ask everyone to not forget, raise their voice, and demand the immediate return of your daughters.

With all my solidarity,
Your friend and father of Malala, Ziauddin Yousafzai.

60

Mayor of Los Angeles Eric Garcetti et al.'s Letter to Donald Trump on Climate Change, 2016

Having tweeted in 2012 that he believed the 'concept of global warming was created by and for the Chinese in order to make US manufacturing non-competitive', Donald Trump's first major speech on energy policy as the Republican presidential nominee in May 2016 contained a commitment to 'cancel' the Paris climate deal if he ever became president, and a call for more oil and gas drilling and less regulation around fossil fuels, ambitions that he reiterated through his successful campaign.

In the wake of his electoral victory in November of the same year, the mayors of seventy-one US cities composed the following letter in an attempt to persuade him to take another look at the issue.

22 November, 2016

Dear President-elect Trump,

As Mayors, we have taken it upon ourselves to take bold action within our cities to tackle the climate crisis head-on. We write today to ask for your partnership in our work to clean our air, strengthen our economy, and ensure that our children inherit a nation healthier and better prepared for the future than it is today.

We lead 71 small and large American cities, comprising nearly 38 million Americans in both blue and red states. We have joined together in the U.S. Mayors' National Climate Action Agenda (MNCAA), or the #ClimateMayors, in addressing the greatest challenge of our time, climate change. Each of our cities is committing to ambitious targets to reduce greenhouse gas emissions, set climate action, regularly report on our progress, share lessons and hold each other accountable. Around the globe, cities are working together through organizations like C40 as well.

The effects of climate change – extreme storms, wildfires and drought; sea level rise and storm surge; choking air pollution in cities; disruption of agricultural supply chains and jobs in rural heartlands; and coastal erosion, to name a few – are a clear and present danger to American interests at home and abroad. This is why the U.S. Department of Defense stated in 2015 "that climate change is an urgent and growing threat to our national security". Furthermore, estimates have shown these impacts from climate change could cost the American economy $500 billion annually by 2050, and that figure will only rise unless we work together to stem, and ultimately reverse, the amount of greenhouse gases entering our atmosphere.

The cost of prevention pales in comparison to cost of inaction, in terms of dollars, property and human life. As our incoming President, as a businessman, and as a parent, we believe we can find common ground when it comes to addressing an issue not rooted in politics or philosophy, but in science and hard economic data. Simply put, we can all agree that fires, flooding and financial losses are bad for our country, that we need to protect our communities' most vulnerable residents who suffer the most from the impacts of climate change, and that we all need healthier air to breathe and a stronger economy – rural and urban, Republican and Democrat – and in terms of our domestic quality of life and our standing abroad.

On November 8, American voters approved more than $200 billion in local measures, funded by their own local tax dollars, to improve quality of life and reduce carbon pollution. Seventy percent of voters in Los Angeles County, the car capital of the world, approved a $120 billion, multi-decade commitment to public transit. Seattle voters approved transit investments totaling $54 billion; Austin voters approved a record-setting $720 million mobility bond; Boston voters approved investment in affordable housing, parks, historic preservation and more.

As President, you will have the power to expand and accelerate these local initiatives which the people resoundingly supported. We call upon you and the federal government you will lead to help cities leverage funds for the hundreds of billions of dollars in transit, energy, infrastructure and real estate development necessary to upgrade our infrastructure for the 21st century. We ask that you lead us in expanding the renewable energy sources we need to achieve energy security, address climate change and spark a new manufacturing, energy and construction boom in America. We ask that you help provide American businesses the certainty to invest through continued tax credits for electric vehicles, solar power, renewables and other clean technologies. And we ask that you shift to embrace the Paris Climate Agreement and make US cities your partner in doing so.

While we are prepared to forge ahead even in the absence of federal support, we know that if we stand united on this issue, we can make change that will resonate for generations. We have no choice and no room to doubt our resolve. The time for bold leadership and action is now.

Signed,
Mayor Eric Garcetti
City of Los Angeles, CA

Mayor Martin J Walsh
City of Boston, MA

Mayor Bill de Blasio
New York City, NY et al.

61

Patrick Millsaps' Open Letter to Ariana Grande on the Manchester Terrorist Attack, 2017

On 22 May 2017, twenty-two people, including an eight-year-old girl, lost their lives following an attack on the Manchester Arena by a suicide bomber after a concert by the American singer and actor Ariana Grande. Traumatised by the attack and the deaths of so many of her young fans, Grande stated she was 'broken, from the bottom of my heart' and questioned whether she would be able to sing again. But among the messages she received urging her to carry on, whenever she felt ready, was a letter posted on Twitter by Patrick Millsaps, a father of three daughters who described himself as 'a fat dude in Georgia'.

Millsaps' letter went viral and Ariana appeared at the Old Trafford Cricket Ground a month after the attack, to sing in a charity concert she'd helped organise that raised £10 million for the families of the victims.

24 May 2017

Dear Miss Grande,

I am the father of three daughters – ages 13, 12 & 12. So, you have been part of our family for years. On occasion your songs may have stayed on the radio AFTER I have dropped the girls off at school. I will neither confirm nor deny that I have personally seen every episode of "Sam & Kat."

Since you are a part of our family and after reading a tweet you posted on the Twitter the other night; I'm afraid I need to set you straight girl. So listen up and receive some redneck love from a daddy of daughters.

#1. You don't have a dadgum thing to apologize for. If some jackass had gotten drunk and killed someone with his car next to your hotel in Manchester, would you feel responsible? If the night before your concert, a tornado had hit Manchester and tragically killed several people who were going to go to your concert; would you feel the need to apologize? You see, you are no more responsible for the actions of an insane coward who committed an evil act in your proximity than you would be for a devastating natural disaster or morons near your hotel. Your text was some stinkin' thinkin' in that regard.

#2. In your line of work, you have so many experts who are now "strategizing" what you should do next (I used to be one of those "experts" when I managed talent). Tell them ALL to go take a powder, give them the month off, and tell them that if they call you within the next 30 days, they are fired! These "experts" don't have a freaking clue what you are processing right now. Spend time with your God, your family and your friends who will give you space and support when you need it. Hell, go lick as many freaking donuts as you want. Girl, you deserve it!

#3. When and only when you are ready, on behalf of all dads who love your . . . um . . . whose daughters love your music SING AGAIN. Music is the international language of peace. Every time you open your mouth and share that incredible God-given gift to the world, you make this crappy world a little less crappy.

So there you go my dear, unsolicited advice from a fat dude in Georgia who loves his daughters and appreciate that there are people like you in the world. Take care of you first. Your fans aren't going anywhere.

Sincerely,
Morgan, Alison & Kendall's Daddy

62

Time's Up's Letter to the *New York Times* on Sexual Harassment, 2018

On 5 October 2017 the *New York Times* published an article that revealed multiple allegations of sexual harassment against the Hollywood mogul Harvey Weinstein, dating back decades. In the coming months a slew of further accusations, of harassment and assault, of rape and forced oral sex, followed, as actor after actor came forward, joining the likes of Rose McGowan, Ashley Judd, Annabella Sciorra, Mira Sorvino and Salma Hayek in making the abuse they had suffered at the hands of Weinstein public.* In May 2018, Weinstein was finally indicted on rape and criminal sex act charges in New York.

The 'Weinstein effect' precipitated a much broader and global conversation about power, abuse and equality, with the Twitter hashtag #MeToo encouraging women from all walks of life to share their own experiences of mistreatment and sexual harassment.

In addition, a group of over 300 women in Hollywood, including Hayek, Reese Witherspoon and Natalie Portman, banded together to found Time's Up, an organisation dedicated to improving conditions and promoting greater equality for all women in the workplace.

Responding to an open letter of support posted by Alianza Nacional de Campesinas, the National Farmworker Women's Alliance, on 10 November 2017, Time's Up sent its own open letter to the *New York Times*.

---

* Weinstein continues to 'unequivocally' deny any allegations of non-consensual sex.

December 21, 2017

Dear Sisters,

We write on behalf of [over 1,000] women who work in film, television and theater. A little more than two months ago, courageous individuals revealed the dark truth of ongoing sexual harassment and assault by powerful people in the entertainment industry. At one of our most difficult and vulnerable moments, Alianza Nacional de Campesinas (the National Farmworker Women's Alliance) sent us a powerful and compassionate message of solidarity for which we are deeply grateful.

To the members of *Alianza* and farmworker women across the country, we see you, we thank you, and we acknowledge the heavy weight of our common experience of being preyed upon, harassed, and exploited by those who abuse their power and threaten our physical and economic security. We have similarly suppressed the violence and demeaning harassment for fear that we will be attacked and ruined in the process of speaking. We share your feelings of anger and shame. We harbor fear that no one will believe us, that we will look weak or that we will be dismissed; and we are terrified that we will be fired or never hired again in retaliation.

We also recognize our privilege and the fact that we have access to enormous platforms to amplify our voices. Both of which have drawn and driven widespread attention to the existence of this problem in our industry that farmworker women and countless individuals employed in other industries have not been afforded.

To every woman employed in agriculture who has had to fend off unwanted sexual advances from her boss, every housekeeper who has tried to escape an assaultive guest, every janitor trapped nightly in a building with a predatory supervisor, every waitress grabbed by a customer and expected to take it with a smile, every garment and factory worker forced to trade sexual acts for more shifts, every domestic worker or home health aide forcibly touched by a client, every immigrant woman silenced by the threat of her undocumented status being reported in retaliation for speaking up and to women in every industry who are subjected to indignities and offensive behavior that they are

We want all survivors of sexual harassment, everywhere, to be heard, to be believed, and to know that accountability is possible.

Time's Up

expected to tolerate in order to make a living: We stand with you. We support you.

Now, unlike ever before, our access to the media and to important decision makers has the potential of leading to real accountability and consequences. We want all survivors of sexual harassment, everywhere, to be heard, to be believed, and to know that accountability is possible. We also want all victims and survivors to be able to access justice and support for the wrongdoing they have endured. We particularly want to lift up the voices, power, and strength of women working in low-wage industries where the lack of financial stability makes them vulnerable to high rates of gender-based violence and exploitation.

Unfortunately, too many centers of power – from legislatures to boardrooms to executive suites and management to academia – lack gender parity and women do not have equal decision-making authority. This systemic gender-inequality and imbalance of power fosters an environment that is ripe for abuse and harassment against women. Therefore, we call for a significant increase of women in positions of leadership and power across industries. In addition, we seek equal representation, opportunities, benefits and pay for all women workers, not to mention greater representation of women of color, immigrant women, and lesbian, bisexual, and transgender women, whose experiences in the workforce are often significantly worse than their white, cisgender, straight peers. The struggle for women to break in, to rise up the ranks and to simply be heard and acknowledged in male-dominated workplaces must end; time's up on this impenetrable monopoly.

We are grateful to the many individuals – survivors and allies – who are speaking out and forcing the conversation about sexual harassment, sexual assault, and gender bias out of the shadows and into the spotlight. We fervently urge the media covering the disclosures by people in Hollywood to spend equal time on the myriad experiences of individuals working in less glamorized and valorized trades.

Harassment too often persists because perpetrators and employers never face any consequences. This is often because survivors, particularly those working in low-wage industries, don't have the resources to fight back. As a first step towards helping women and men across the country seek justice, the signatories of this letter will be seeding a legal fund to help survivors of sexual assault and harassment across all industries challenge those responsible for the harm against them and give voice to their experiences.

We remain committed to holding our own workplaces accountable, pushing for swift and effective change to make the entertainment industry a safe and equitable place for everyone, and telling women's stories through our eyes and voices with the goal of shifting our society's perception and treatment of women.

In solidarity,
Abbi Jacobson
Adrienne Warren
Adrienne Houghton et al.

Permissions

The editor and publisher gratefully acknowledge the permission granted to reproduce the copyright material in this book.

p. 59 © The Bertrand Russell Peace Foundation. Permission granted by The Bertrand Russell Peace Foundation. p. 62 from *Wilfred Owen: Collected Letters*, ed. Harold Owen and John Bell, Oxford University Press, 1967. Reprinted with permission of Wilfred Owen Royalties Trust. p. 66 © Siegfried Sassoon by kind permission of the Estate of George Sassoon. p. 89 From *The Standard Edition of the Complete Psychological Works of Sigmund Freud*, translated and edited by James Strachey, *Volume XXII* by Sigmund Freud. Published by Vintage Classics. Reprinted by permission of The Random House Group Limited. Reproduced by permission of Sigmund Freud copyrights/The Marsh Agency Ltd. 'Why War?' (1932-07-30, Archival Call Number 92-350) from The Albert Einstein Archives. Copyright © 1987 – 2018 by The Hebrew University of Jerusalem and Princeton University Press. Reprinted by permission of Princeton University Press. p. 110 From *Letters from Prison* by Antonio Gramsci, translated and edited by Lynne Lawner. Copyright © 1975 by Antonio Gramsci, translated and edited by Lynne Lawner, © 1986 reverted to Lynne Lawner. Reprinted by permission of Georges Borchardt, Inc., on behalf of the author. p. 113 'Letter to Robert Duncan' from *The Diary of Anaïs Nin Volume Three: 1939–1944*, copyright © 1969 by Anaïs Nin and renewed 1997 by Rupert Pole and Gunther Stuhlmann, reprinted by permission of Houghton Mifflin Harcourt Publishing Company, all rights reserved and from *Women's Letters: America from the Revolutionary War to the Present*, copyright © 2008 Edited by Lisa Grunwald and Stephen J. Adler, reprinted by permission of Peter Owen Publishers UK. p. 116 Reproduced with permission of Curtis Brown Group Ltd, London on behalf of The

Estate of the late Lesley Milne Ltd Copyright © A A Milne, 1950. p. 129 'Letter to Noel Willmett Regarding Totalitarianism' by George Orwell (Copyright © George Orwell, 1944); reproduced by permission of Bill Hamilton as the Literary Executor of the Estate of the Late Sonia Brownell Orwell. From *A Life in Letters* by George Orwell. Published by Harvill Secker. Reprinted by permission of The Random House Group Limited. © 2010. p. 139 © Lillian Hellman. Permission kindly granted by the Hellman Trust. p. 147 From *Lost Woods: The Discovered Writing of Rachel Carson.* Copyright © 1998 by Roger Allen Christie. Reprinted by permission of Frances Collin, Trustee. p. 150 'Letter to Picasso' by Czesław Miłosz. Copyright © 1956, Czesław Miłosz, used by permission of The Wylie Agency (UK) Limited. p. 156 copyright © 1997 by Doris Lessing. Featured by kind permission of Jonathan Clowes Ltd, London, on behalf of The Estate of Doris Lessing. p. 164 © The David Graham Du Bois Trust, from the W. E. B. Du Bois Papers, Special Collections and University Archives, University of Massachusetts, Amherst. Permission granted by The David Graham Du Bois Trust. p. 172 Reprinted by arrangement with The Heirs to the Estate of Martin Luther King Jr., c/o Writers House as agent for the proprietor New York, NY. Copyright: © 1963 Dr. Martin Luther King, Jr. © renewed 1991 Coretta Scott King. p. 180 From *And a Voice to Sing With* by Joan Baez. Copyright © 1987 by Joan Baez. Reprinted with the permission of Simon & Schuster, Inc. All rights reserved. p. 192 © Ron Ridenhour. Permission granted by The Nation Institute. p. 205 © Red Saunders. Permission kindly granted by the author. p. 208 'Letter to Mama' [pp. 221–3] from *More Tales of the City* by Armistead Maupin. Copyright © 1979 by The Chronicle Publishing Company. Reprinted by permission of HarperCollins Publishers. p. 211 courtesy: Jimmy Carter Presidential Library. p. 213 © Women's Peace Camp. Permission granted by West Berkshire Museum. p. 217 Courtesy of the Olusegun Obasanjo Presidential Library, Presidential Boulevard Way, Oke Mosan, Abeokuta, Ogun State, Nigeria. p. 221 © Alex Molnar, permission kindly granted by the author. p. 225 © Orlando & Phyllis Rodriguez. Permission kindly granted by the authors. p. 238 From *Letters to My Grandchildren* by Tony Benn. Published by

Hutchinson. Reprinted by permission of The Random House Group Limited. © 2009. p. 240 © Stephen Fry. Permission granted by David Higham Associates. p. 244 © Edward Snowden. Permission granted by the author. p. 249 © Ziauddin Yousafzai. Permission granted by Curtis Brown. p. 251 © Aaron Parsons. Permission granted by Aaron Parsons. p. 254 © Patrick Millsaps. Permission granted by Patrick Millsaps.

Every effort has been made to trace copyright holders and to obtain their permission for the use of copyright material. The publisher apologises for any errors or omissions in the above list and would be grateful if notified of any corrections that should be incorporated in future reprints or editions of this book.